I0427753

COMBATING HUMAN TRAFFICKING IN OUR MAJOR CITIES

FIELD HEARING

BEFORE THE

COMMITTEE ON HOMELAND SECURITY
HOUSE OF REPRESENTATIVES

ONE HUNDRED THIRTEENTH CONGRESS

SECOND SESSION

MARCH 20, 2014

Serial No. 113–57

Printed for the use of the Committee on Homeland Security

Available via the World Wide Web: http://www.gpo.gov/fdsys/

U.S. GOVERNMENT PRINTING OFFICE

88–557 PDF   WASHINGTON : 2014

For sale by the Superintendent of Documents, U.S. Government Printing Office
Internet: bookstore.gpo.gov   Phone: toll free (866) 512–1800; DC area (202) 512–1800
Fax: (202) 512–2250   Mail: Stop SSOP, Washington, DC 20402–0001

(II)

CONTENTS

(III)

IV

FOR THE RECORD

COMBATING HUMAN TRAFFICKING IN OUR MAJOR CITIES

Thursday, March 20, 2014

U.S. HOUSE OF REPRESENTATIVES,
COMMITTEE ON HOMELAND SECURITY,
Houston, TX.

The committee met, pursuant to call, at 10:00 a.m., in Auditorium Room 116, Roderick R. Paige Education Building, College of Education, Texas Southern University, Houston, Texas, Hon. Michael T. McCaul [Chairman of the committee] presiding.

Present: Representatives McCaul and Jackson Lee.

Also present: Representatives Poe, Farenthold, Gene Green of Texas, and Al Green of Texas.

Chairman McCAUL. We are proud to be here and also Al Green, an alumni of this institution, as well.

I also want to thank State representative Allen Fletcher. I do not know where he is out there. He serves as vice chairman of the Homeland Security Committee in the State legislature, does a great job, former Houston police officer, and also was appointed to the Texas legislature's Joint Committee to Study Human Trafficking and has a very keen interest in the subject matter. We thank you, sir, for your leadership at the State level.

Last but not least, I cannot go forward without also recognizing the queen of Houston, Joanne Herring, who is joining us today. It is a real honor to have you.

[Applause.]

Chairman McCAUL. I could go on and on about her background, but I think we all know her so well. Thank you so much for being here today.

So with that, the Committee on Homeland Security will come to order.

The committee is meeting today to examine our Nation's efforts to combat human trafficking. I want to thank everybody, including the witnesses, for attending this important hearing today.

I appreciate the effort taken on behalf of those involved to put this hearing together. This is an official Congressional hearing, as opposed to a town hall meeting, and as such, we must abide by the rules of the Committee on Homeland Security and of the House of Representatives. There are some admonitions about applause and that sort of thing, but I think I will skip that and move on. But decorum of the committee, obviously, is important here today.

Before I recognize myself for an opening statement, I ask unanimous consent that the gentleman from Texas, Mr. Poe; the gentleman from Texas, Mr. Farenthold; the gentleman from Texas, Mr.

Gene Green; and the gentleman from Texas, Mr. Al Green—this is great to have an all-Texas panel, I got to tell you—be permitted to sit on the dais and participate in today's hearing. Without objection, so ordered.

I now recognize myself for an opening statement.

We are here today in the heart of Houston, a metropolitan area of nearly 6 million people. The city has a thriving international community, the second-busiest port in the country, and this is a major center for commerce, not far from the Mexican border. It is known for hosting high-profile events, including the upcoming Super Bowl in 2017. Sadly, many of the things that make Houston an attractive place to live and do business also make it a major hub for the tragic business of human trafficking.

In this city and many other cities across the United States, women and children, some not even in their teens, are held against their will and forced into prostitution rings. Children who should be learning in school, as we sit here, are also held captive and forced into manual labor, along with their parents, in order to satisfy exorbitant illegal debts to traffickers that they can never hope to repay. Some are brought into the United States from abroad with the promise of freedom and opportunity, only to be forced into modern-day slavery. As a father of five children, I cannot imagine that kind of situation.

However, many are American citizens. They live in difficult conditions. Some are abandoned or homeless or runaways, and they trust the first person who offers them a way out. Often this person is a trafficker, a person that is an expert on detecting vulnerability and a master at exploitation. Human trafficking is emerging in epidemic proportions throughout the United States and the world. While victims might not be physically imprisoned, they are trapped in deplorable conditions through force, fraud, or coercion that can make escape seem impossible.

As the fastest-growing criminal industry, it is generating billions of dollars for its perpetrators every day. Hundreds of thousands of American children have become victims of human trafficking. In Texas, the Office of the Attorney General reported that between 2007 and 2012, it identified almost 700 human trafficking-related incidences, involving almost 800 victims. Yet, even with stats like these, it still comes as a surprise to many people just how prevalent and close to home human trafficking has become.

Today, however, there is hope. One of our witnesses today entered the world of sex trafficking at age 12, which is utterly amazing and shocking and horrifying. Now decades later, she is working to rescue girls in the same situation.

The Houston area has identified the problem and is making great strides towards prevention and eradication of trafficking. The Human Trafficking Rescue Alliance was formed in 2004 to bring together a range of law enforcement and victim service partners that traditionally would not have the opportunity to work together. In 2003, Texas was one of the leading States to enact a robust State trafficking law and has recently formed a task force to combat trafficking and rescue and restore those that fall victim to it.

At the Federal level, the Human Smuggling and Trafficking Center serves as a clearinghouse for all information related to human smuggling and trafficking. The Department of Homeland Security's lead investigative unit is within the Immigration and Customs Enforcement. In 2010, DHS formed the Blue Campaign, a combined effort to provide enhanced public awareness, training, victim assistance, and criminal investigations. DHS, the Department of Justice, and the State Department have collaborated with Mexican law enforcement counterparts on the U.S./Mexico Human Trafficking Bilateral Enforcement Initiative. Through this initiative, both governments have developed high-impact bilateral investigations and prosecutions aimed at dismantling international human trafficking networks.

Despite this collaboration, human trafficking is still far too prevalent and requires a coordinated effort from every available organization and resource to fight the problem. I am proud to cosponsor my friend and colleague, Congressman Ted Poe—his one bill, the End Sex Slavery Act, and his second one, Justice for Victims of Trafficking Act. These bills will address a number of gaps in human trafficking laws and provide much needed support to victims.

I am grateful for the survivors who have bravely agreed to share their story here today, and I look forward to hearing from our other witnesses on their experiences in combating human trafficking. It is my hope that with the help of your testimony, we will raise awareness about this issue and identify solutions that will have a significant impact on human trafficking in Houston and throughout this Nation.

[The statement of Chairman McCaul follows:]

STATEMENT OF CHAIRMAN MICHAEL T. McCAUL

MARCH 20, 2014

We are here today in the heart of Houston; a metropolitan area of nearly 6 million people. This city has a thriving international community, the second-busiest port in the country, and is a major center for commerce not far from the Mexican border. It is known for hosting high-profile events including the Super Bowl in 2017. Sadly, many of the things that make Houston an attractive place to live and do business also make it a major hub for the tragic business of human trafficking.

In this city, and many other cities across the United States, women and children, some not even in their teens, are held against their will and forced into prostitution rings. Children, who should be learning in school as we sit here, are also held captive and forced into manual labor along with their parents, in order to satisfy exorbitant illegal debts to traffickers that they can never hope to repay. Some are brought into the United States from abroad with the promise of freedom and opportunity only to be forced into modern-day slavery. As a father of five children, I cannot imagine that situation.

However, many are American citizens. They live in difficult conditions—some are abandoned or homeless or runaways—and they trust the first person who offers them a way out. Often this person is a trafficker, a person that is an expert on detecting vulnerability, and a master at exploitation. Human trafficking is emerging in epidemic proportions throughout the United States and the world. While victims might not be physically imprisoned, they are trapped in deplorable conditions through force, fraud, or coercion that can make escape seem impossible.

As the fastest-growing criminal industry, it is generating billions of dollars for its perpetrators every year. Hundreds of thousands of American children have become victims of human trafficking. In Texas, the Office of the Attorney General reported that between 2007 and 2012, it identified almost 700 human trafficking-related incidences, involving almost 800 victims. Yet even with statistics like these, it still comes as a surprise to many people just how prevalent and close to home human trafficking has become.

Today, however, there is hope. One of our witnesses today entered the world of sex trafficking at age 12. Now, decades later, she is working to rescue girls in the same situation.

The Houston area has identified the problem and is making great strides towards prevention and eradication of trafficking. The Human Trafficking Rescue Alliance was formed in 2004 to bring together a range of law enforcement and victim service partners that traditionally would not have the opportunity to work together. In 2003, Texas was one of the leading States to enact a robust State trafficking law and has recently formed a task force to combat trafficking and rescue and restore those that fall victim to it.

At the Federal level, the Human Smuggling and Trafficking Center serves as a clearinghouse for all information related to human smuggling and trafficking. The Department of Homeland Security's lead investigative unit is within Immigration and Customs Enforcement. In 2010, DHS formed the Blue Campaign, a combined effort to provide enhanced public awareness, training, victim assistance, and criminal investigations. DHS, the Department of Justice, and the State Department have collaborated with Mexican law enforcement counterparts on the U.S./Mexico Human Trafficking Bilateral Enforcement Initiative. Through this initiative, both governments have developed high-impact bilateral investigations and prosecutions aimed at dismantling international human trafficking networks.

Despite this collaboration, human trafficking is still far too prevalent and requires a coordinated effort from every available organization and resource to fight the problem. I am proud to co-sponsor Congressman Ted Poe's End Sex Slavery Act and his Justice for Victims of Trafficking Act. These bills will address a number of gaps in human trafficking laws and provide much-needed support to victims.

I am grateful for the survivors who have bravely agreed to share their story, and I look forward to hearing from our other witnesses on their experiences in combating human trafficking. It is my hope that with the help of your testimony, we will raise awareness about this issue and identify solutions that will have a significant impact on human trafficking in Houston and throughout the Nation.

Chairman MCCAUL. The Chairman now recognizes the acting Ranking Member, the gentlelady from Texas, Ms. Jackson Lee, for any opening statement she may have.

Ms. JACKSON LEE. Mr. Chairman, thank you for holding today's hearing on the issue of human trafficking in our major cities and just a brief moment of personal privilege to thank Texas Southern University. Dean Holley, thank you, the Dean of the Thurgood Marshall School of Law, to the dean of this school and to the dean of the School of Education and the dean of the School of Public Affairs, Mr. LaRence Snowden, and the president, President Rudley, and the regents. Let me thank you for the hospitality that you have offered us at a very historic institution.

Might I also thank and welcome again the many witnesses who accepted our invitation to be here and for the work we have done together.

Finally, the Chairman has already acknowledged Joanne Herring. He did not give her vitae. But all I will say to you is that she was on the early front lines of saving boys and girls in Afghanistan and in this Nation from the devastation of sexual exploitation and exploitation as it relates to their human rights. So welcome, Ms. Herring, and your very special guests as well.

I am the Ranking Member of the Border and Maritime Security Subcommittee and have studied this issue from the connection in the Judiciary Committee to the fact that people traffic across borders, and I could not imagine being silent on this issue and particularly knowing the front lines that Texas and Texas law enforcement and social and civic leaders are involved in this issue. Knowing the magnitude of the problem in the State of Texas, and the Houston area in particular, I requested this hearing shortly after my colleague from Texas became Chairman of the Committee on

Homeland Security. Again, I thank him. I am very pleased that he agreed to my request and that we could come together on a bipartisan basis today to convene the hearing.

Again, I also thank the Ranking Member, Mr. Thompson, and his staff for their cooperation with the Majority on this hearing.

I also appreciate my other colleagues for joining us, and I welcome them to my Congressional——

[Audio disruption.]

Ms. JACKSON LEE [continuing]. For this particular committee being broadcast on the Homeland Security website, and it will become a part of the committee's record for the 113th Congress.

To understand why I believe so strongly that the Committee on Homeland Security should hold this hearing in Houston, you just have to turn on the news yesterday or pick up today's paper. Yesterday morning, law enforcement officials raided a stash house in southeast Houston and found more than 100 people, in fact, 115 people. Nineteen of them are juveniles, all presumed to be in the United States without documentation, being kept inside in squalid conditions. Although the investigation is not complete and there is not a suggestion yet of human trafficking, we note that there are 19 juveniles, and we do not know the destinations of any of those who have been smuggled. What were they here for? What were they intending to do? Among the group were a number of women, including at least one of whom was pregnant, but we do know a number of children.

While all the circumstances surrounding this situation are not yet known, it is obvious that criminal organizations are trafficking or smuggling large groups of people through our community, putting their victims' welfare at risk. We see these tragic news stories all too frequently in our community. For example, a story from January of this year about a notorious Port of Houston area cantina that functioned for years as a center for human trafficking and prostitution. Or another story from earlier this year where a Houston area trafficking ring had been bringing people into the country illegally from Mexico and Central America and sending them to work at restaurants for 12 hours a day, 6 hours a day for very little money. Or a story from last fall where Federal agents arrested suspects in connection with an alleged sex trafficking ring in Houston that prostituted underage, undocumented girls from Mexico who were locked up and beaten by their traffickers.

As a large city strategically located near the border, a major port and a critical transportation corridor, Houston is an attractive target for human trafficking organizations. The statistics support this unfortunate fact. For example, approximately 25 percent of human trafficking cases in the United States are located in Texas and most of those occur in Houston. One of our witnesses today will tell of her prostitution and how it led her to the introduction to human trafficking.

In recent years, 30 percent of calls received from the National Human Trafficking Hotline were out of Texas.

The U.S. Department of Justice has identified the I–10 corridor as the No. 1 trafficking route in the United States.

One of every three runaways in Texas is lured into sex trafficking within 48 hours of leaving home.

Nationally the Federal Government estimates as many as 17,500 people are trafficked to this country each year, for reliable estimates are hard to come by due to the covert nature of the crime and under-reporting of victims, which can lead to the scourge of modern-day slavery where people are held against their will to perform a service. There are likely far more individuals being exploited by traffickers in places where they cannot be readily identified or counted. Exacerbating this problem is the fact that many trafficked victims come from the most vulnerable populations, children, women, and the undocumented.

Understanding the scope and seriousness of the human trafficking problem in Houston and across Texas and throughout the country, the important question remains: How can we fix this? Clearly it will take cooperation from all stakeholders to address the complex issues involved. Legislators, law enforcement officers, health care professionals, victims assistance organizations, and advocacy groups all have a vital role to play. We have brought together these stakeholders today to testify about their current efforts, as well as what more needs to be done, to address the scourge of human trafficking. And as a senior Member of the Homeland Security Committee, I am particularly interested in hearing from the witness from the U.S. Immigration and Customs Enforcement, ICE, on his agency's efforts to combat human trafficking and what Congress can do more.

I believe Homeland Security should be front and center on the front lines of this crucial scourge to eliminate it.

I thank the Chairman for coming to offer us a frank discussion, and as we support and recognize my colleague on the Judiciary Committee, Mr. Poe, we work together on this issue and his legislation dealing with the criminality of it—I believe it is also important to have the Homeland Security Committee have its stake and be a stakeholder as well. We are drafting, as we speak, an omnibus bill dealing with a number of issues to reinforce those front-liners to stop human trafficking once and for all in its tracks because as Americans, we simply cannot allow human trafficking, a form of modern-day slavery, to exist in our country.

Again, I thank the Chairman for holding today's hearing. It is my pleasure to join you and my colleagues. I especially thank you for your presence here today.

I yield back my time.

Chairman McCAUL. I thank the Ranking Member.

Before I introduce the witnesses, I ask unanimous consent that a statement from the Department of Homeland Security's Blue Campaign and a statement from the Department of Justice be included in the record. Without objection, so ordered.

[The information follows:]

STATEMENT OF THE DEPARTMENT OF HOMELAND SECURITY

MARCH 20, 2014

INTRODUCTION

The Department of Homeland Security (DHS) welcomes and appreciates the opportunity to submit this testimony for the record. The men and women of DHS are dedicated to combating the heinous crime of human trafficking using the programs and authorities provided to us by Congress and the President. The Department's Blue Campaign coordinates and unites this work.

DHS recognizes that fighting the hidden crime of human trafficking is a collaborative effort. DHS depends on strong partnerships with other Federal agencies, foreign governments, international organizations, law enforcement, first responders, the faith-based community, non-profit organizations, the private sector, as well as our State, local, and Tribal counterparts. The President's Interagency Task Force to Monitor and Combat Trafficking in Persons (PITF) and the Senior Policy Operating Group (SPOG) bring together Federal departments and agencies, including DHS, to ensure a whole-of-Government approach that addresses all aspects of human trafficking. DHS also co-chairs the SPOG victim services working group along with the Department of Justice and Health and Human Services, which is responsible for leading development of the Federal Strategic Action Plan on Services for Victims of Human Trafficking in the United States. We forged additional partnerships that unite and amplify our joint efforts. DHS greatly appreciates the collaboration and commitment of its partners.

BLUE CAMPAIGN

DHS is one of the lead Federal law enforcement agencies responsible for investigating and preventing human trafficking. Our investigative authority, screening authority, and most of our assistance programs are authorized under the Trafficking Victims Protection Act (TVPA) and the subsequent reauthorizations.

DHS and its components work to combat human trafficking every day. U.S. Immigration Customs Enforcement (ICE) investigates both international and domestic human trafficking cases. U.S. Citizenship and Immigration Services (USCIS) and ICE provide immigration relief to trafficking victims. The Federal Law Enforcement Training Center (FLETC) provides training to law enforcement professionals on how to identify indicators of human trafficking and how to conduct human trafficking investigations. The Office of Intelligence and Analysis (I&A) facilitates training and webinars to State and major urban area fusion centers on the signs and indicators of human trafficking and the April 18, 2013 Fusion Center protocol for reporting. U.S. Customs and Border Protection (CBP) is in a unique position to detect trafficking on our borders, as are the U.S. Coast Guard (USCG) on the high seas, the Transportation Security Administration (TSA) at airports and mass transit facilities, and the Federal Emergency Management Agency (FEMA) in disaster areas.

DHS unites these missions under the Blue Campaign to combat human trafficking. Blue is the international color of human trafficking awareness, and the Blue Campaign name references the global anti-human trafficking symbols of the Blue Heart and the Blue Blindfold, as well as the "thin blue line" of law enforcement. To increase awareness of this crime domestically and internationally, in June 2010, then-Secretary of Homeland Security Janet Napolitano launched the Blue Campaign.

Before we talk about the Blue Campaign, we would like to share a story that demonstrates why DHS cares so deeply about human trafficking. When Shyima Hall was 8 years old, her parents sold her into slavery. She was smuggled into the United States when she was 10 years old. She worked as a domestic servant in Orange County, California, 16 hour days, scrubbing floors, cooking meals and cleaning house. She was rarely allowed outside. She never went to school. She never visited a doctor or dentist and did not speak English. When she was 13, a concerned neighbor called in a tip to law enforcement and ICE opened an investigation. Her captors were prosecuted, imprisoned, and then deported. In 2012, Shyima became a U.S. citizen. She is now 23 years old and has said that her dream is to become an ICE Special Agent, in order to help others in similar situations. Shyima's story helps us understand the important role the Government can play in identifying, investigating, and prosecuting human trafficking. However, we only found out about Shyima because a neighbor called in a tip. Human trafficking is a hidden crime—and every one of us needs to know the indicators to look for.

TRAINING AND OUTREACH

The Blue Campaign was begun, and continues, with no direct appropriations, reflecting a belief that we are all more effective when we work collaboratively with our internal and external partners. Early in the campaign, we developed training to ensure that those in our workforce who encounter potential victims of human trafficking understood the indicators of trafficking. We also created specialized training for the Federal contractor workforce. Federal regulations create a zero tolerance for Government contractors who traffic persons. In response, DHS launched specialized training for acquisition officers about human trafficking that provides information about penalties for traffickers who execute business contracts with the U.S. Government.

We brought all of our components together to make sure our efforts increased identification of and assistance to victims of trafficking. As part of their efforts through the Blue Campaign, DHS components conduct trainings and webinars, produce informational videos, develop informational materials, provide victim assistance, conduct investigative efforts, and conduct outreach.

The Blue Campaign utilizes academic research to shape the focus of the campaign. A recent Northeastern University study noted that few municipal and county agencies had human trafficking training or investigated human trafficking cases. An Urban Institute study found a significant lack of awareness among law enforcement and a lack of prioritization which resulted in many cases being passed over by State and county legal systems.

State and Local Outreach

We created a specialized training to educate law enforcement officers at all levels on the indicators of human trafficking, how they can assist victims, and the resources available to them when investigating such cases. In addition, we developed training videos for State, local, county, Tribal, and territorial law enforcement to create awareness that immigration relief options are potentially available to foreign victims of human trafficking and how these benefits aid law enforcement in achieving successful investigations.

The Blue Campaign also works with our Federal Government colleagues, foreign governments, international organizations, law enforcement at all levels, non-governmental organizations (NGOs), the faith-based community, the private sector, and the general public to share ideas and resources and build a force-multiplying network of diverse but complementary parts. Partnerships augment our efforts by bringing together diverse experiences, amplifying messages, and leveraging resources. Together we can effectively combat human trafficking, by making sure that people understand the crime, recognize its indicators, and know how to seek help and report tips.

Federal Outreach

DHS, along with the Departments of Justice and Labor, partnered to create an advanced human trafficking training course that brings together agents and prosecutors to work on investigating and prosecuting these crimes. This interactive course focuses on complex issues of human trafficking: Search warrants, witness interviewing techniques, immigration relief, evidence gathering, and discovery issues.

International Outreach

We also took new steps to expand our international law enforcement engagement. On October 8, 2012, Secretary Napolitano signed an agreement with INTERPOL Secretary General Ron Noble to allow INTERPOL to place its logo on Blue Campaign materials and distribute them to all 190 member countries. DHS and INTERPOL will work together to share training and awareness materials and best practices, strengthen support for victims, increase regional partnerships, and enhance cooperation on combating human trafficking.

The Blue Campaign also utilizes the expertise and feedback from its community stakeholders and partners to shape the focus of the campaign's efforts. The Blue Campaign meets bi-annually with Federal, State, local, Tribal, non-governmental and community organizations, emergency management and medical professionals, and private-sector partners to receive feedback and guide future initiatives.

Awareness Products

Many stakeholders emphasized that misconceptions about the nature of trafficking exist widely. A common misconception about human trafficking is that it only occurs outside the United States, or if it does occur domestically the victims are all noncitizens. In order to educate the public that human trafficking exists in every country, including the United States, the Blue Campaign developed a series of posters that depict different forms of human trafficking and produced a Public Service Announcement (PSA) titled, "Out of the Shadows." These posters and PSA emphasize that victims can be many types of people, such as young children, women, men, U.S. citizens, new immigrants, and that they come from all socioeconomic groups.

To address the lack of general awareness and training available for non-law enforcement communities and individuals, the Blue Campaign collaborated with the Department of State and other Federal agencies to create a 15-minute general awareness training to educate the public on the indicators of human trafficking and how to report it. DHS also developed cards, posters, and pamphlets that list the indicators of human trafficking and provide a hotline number to those who need help or want to report a suspected trafficking case. These materials are available in 17 languages to meet the language access needs identified by stakeholders and victim assistance information.

The stakeholders also identified the need for more specific information tailored for their communities that listed the tools and resources applicable to their role in fighting human trafficking. The Blue Campaign developed hand-out materials with tailored messages for NGOs, faith-based organizations, law enforcement, judges and lawyers, first responders, and health care professionals to educate about victim identification and crime reporting, the case investigation process, and available resources for victim support.

We also recognize that first responders and health care professionals are in a unique position to identify victims. We produced an informational video to help first responders—including firefighters and emergency medical technicians—identify possible victims of human trafficking, and created indicator cards and posters geared to those professionals. We continue to conduct briefings and webinars at the request of local and National medical first responder groups and associations.

PARTNERSHIPS

Over the past 3 years, the Blue Campaign developed a variety of trainings and materials, and through our partnerships we have been able to expand them to new audiences and support the efforts of our Government and private-sector partners.

Most recently, on September 17, 2013, the Blue Campaign announced a partnership with Western Union. Western Union agents are in a unique position to recognize human trafficking and other illicit activity of criminal organizations and businesses that utilize alternative financing mechanisms to move and store money. Through this alliance, Western Union will provide the Blue Campaign's multilingual training and awareness materials to select agent locations in the Southwest Border region of the United States and certain other high-risk locations. These materials highlight the signs of human trafficking and how to accurately report them. Participating agents will also receive additional training from Western Union on how to detect a potential human trafficking victim and how to involve law enforcement.

Engaging with all levels of government is a priority for the Blue Campaign. The Blue Campaign is pursuing partnerships with National associations representing State, local, Tribal and territorial elected and appointed officials. In July 2013, DHS entered into a partnership agreement with the National Association of Counties (NACo) to promote awareness of human trafficking through the Blue Campaign. NACo is the only National organization that represents county governments in the United States and provides essential services to the Nation's 3,069 counties. Through this partnership, DHS will deliver webinar training, share resources to bring awareness about human trafficking and co-brand public awareness materials with both Blue Campaign and NACo logos.

We partnered with the U.S. Department of Transportation (DOT) to enhance awareness and victim identification to the transportation industry. DOT adapted the Blue Campaign's awareness training to their workforce and in 2012, nearly all 55,000 of its employees have taken the course.

In 2012, DHS, DOT, and Amtrak entered a partnership to train all 20,000 Amtrak employees and Amtrak Police Department officers to identify and recognize indicators of human trafficking, as well as how to report suspected cases of human trafficking. We also work with the airline industry to think strategically about how it can assist in victim identification. CBP, together with DOT launched the Blue Lightning Initiative, a training program to educate airline employees how to identify human trafficking in airports or during flights and how to notify law enforcement. Since the Blue Lightning Initiative rollout, five airlines have committed to use the Blue Lightning Initiative: Delta, JetBlue, Allegiant, Silver Airways, and North American.

The initial partnership with DOT led to further collaborations and joint partnerships with transportation industries. DHS and DOT provided the training to approximately 6,000 State and local law enforcement, including investigators at the Federal Motor Carrier Safety Administration, on the best ways to detect human trafficking on trucks and buses, and these trainings will continue.

These partnerships and outreach are leading directly to more tips, more investigations, and improved services for victims, and will help us achieve our ultimate goal of supporting successful prosecutions and deterrence.

INVESTIGATIONS AND VICTIM SUPPORT

In fiscal year 2012, ICE Homeland Security Investigations (HSI) Tip Line (1–866–347–2423) received more human trafficking tips than ever before, receiving 588 tips—up from 384 in fiscal year 2011 and 231 in fiscal year 2010.

We investigate hundreds of human trafficking cases each year and work with the Department of Justice to ensure cases are successfully prosecuted. In fiscal year 2012, ICE HSI investigated more cases with a nexus to human trafficking than ever before, resulting in 894 initiated cases, 381 convictions, and seized assets of more than $1,000,000. We take a victim-centered approach in our investigations and have Victim Assistance Specialists across the ICE offices all over the United States. In recognition of the needs and unique challenges of interviewing trafficked minors and other child and special needs victims, DHS expanded its Forensic Interviewing Program to five full-time Forensic Interview Specialists.

We have observed an increase in the correlation between human trafficking and gang activity. We know that some gang members work directly with non-gang trafficking organizations. For example, gang members provide "security" enforcements at certain brothels.

Gangs have now added human trafficking to their existing crimes of drugs and firearm trafficking. Gangs recruit young girls and compel them to commit acts of commercial sex. This has occurred right here in Washington, DC. ICE in collaboration with the Northern Virginia Human Trafficking Task Force and our Federal partners recently investigated and successfully prosecuted cases where MS–13 gang members in Washington, DC, Prince George's County, MD, and Alexandria, VA, recruited girls as young as 12 near schools, on the street, at house parties, and through social media into sex trafficking.

These joint efforts resulted in a life sentence of a MS–13 gang member that sex trafficked a 12-year-old runaway whom he met at a party in Prince George's County, Maryland. The 12-year-old runaway asked for his help in finding a place to stay, and the very next day he was selling her for sex acts in Washington, DC and surrounding counties. For 3 months the MS–13 member sexually exploited the victim for money every day of the week. The trafficker also admitted to having sex with the victim and allowed MS–13 gang members to have sex with her free of charge.

DHS also provides immigration relief to eligible foreign trafficking victims, a critical component to ensuring victim participation for the successful investigation and prosecution of human trafficking cases. There are three forms of immigration relief available for victims of human trafficking—Continued Presence, T visas, and U visas. DHS has streamlined its training about immigration relief for victims to increase awareness among law enforcement agencies. These short- and long-term relief options assist law enforcement in stabilizing victims so that the victim can begin to recover and rebuild his or her life.

We are proud of what DHS has accomplished, but there is much to do still. We are working more every day to expand our partnerships, and we interact regularly with our stakeholders for new ideas and new innovative ways to combat this crime.

In closing, we will continue to work hard to develop our initiatives to meet the needs of victims, law enforcement, and service providers. We are committed to providing quality information, trainings, and products that give communities the information they need to fight human trafficking.

We appreciate the opportunity to represent the Blue Campaign and DHS before the committee.

————

STATEMENT OF THE DEPARTMENT OF JUSTICE

MARCH 20, 2014

Thank you for the opportunity to present an overview of the work of the Department of Justice (the Department) and its Federal Bureau of Investigation (FBI) to combat the scourge of human trafficking. As evidenced by the broad spectrum of investigative, prosecutorial, training, outreach, victim services, and research efforts by a wide array of components, outlined below, the Department is fully committed to fighting human trafficking.

Human trafficking, also known as trafficking in persons or modern-day slavery, is a crime that strikes at the very heart of the American promise: Freedom. Today, in this country, people are bought, sold, and exploited like slaves each and every day. They are trapped in lives of misery—often beaten, starved, and forced to engage in prostitution or to take grueling jobs as migrant, domestic, restaurant, or factory workers with little or no pay.

The most vulnerable among us, including our children, are being exploited both on-line and in person. Often targeted because of individual vulnerabilities, many have already experienced abusive or troubled families, have disabilities, or come from families with very limited resources. In the hands of their traffickers, these individuals will be subjected to numerous sexual assaults and continued abuse.

The Department and its partners are working hard to identify and support victims and bring their abusers to justice. We provide significant resources, training, and technical assistance to our Federal, State, local, and Tribal partners.

ENFORCEMENT: INVESTIGATION

The FBI's efforts to investigate human trafficking are coordinated by the Civil Rights Unit (CRU) and the Violent Crimes Against Children Section (VCACS). The CRU investigates forced labor, sex trafficking by force, fraud, or coercion and the sexual exploitation of foreign minors while the VCACS focuses on the commercial sexual exploitation of domestic children under the age of 18. Sex trafficking prosecutions involving children do not require proof of the use of force, fraud, or coercion.

Innocence Lost National Initiative

This year marks the tenth anniversary of the FBI's most prominent initiative to combat the growing problem of sex trafficking of children within the United States. In June 2003, the FBI and the Department's Child Exploitation and Obscenity Section (CEOS) joined the National Center for Missing and Exploited Children (NCMEC) to launch the Innocence Lost National Initiative (ILNI). While it is difficult to imagine, the average age of a child targeted for prostitution in the United States is between 11 and 14 years old. Once under the control of a pimp, the proceeds of the commercial sexual exploitation of the child are controlled by the captor, and attempted escapes often result in brutal beatings or even death.

The FBI and its ILNI partners execute Operation Cross Country—a 3-day Nationwide enforcement action focusing on underage victims of prostitution. Our most recent operation in July 2013—our seventh and largest such operation—concluded with the recovery of 105 commercially sexually-exploited children and the arrests of 150 pimps and other individuals.

This most recent sweep took place in 76 cities and was carried out by the FBI in partnership with local, State, and Federal law enforcement agencies and NCMEC. Over 1,300 law enforcement officers across the country have been trained through the Protecting Victims of Child Prostitution Course at NCMEC, which supports the ILNI.

Task force operations can begin as local actions, targeting such places as truck stops, casinos, street "tracks," and internet websites, based on intelligence gathered by officers working in their respective jurisdictions. The FBI has developed special teams and protocols for prevention and enforcement actions surrounding large-scale sporting events and other events of National interest. By utilizing information obtained through these operations, and by building a strong rapport with victims, the FBI often uncovers organized efforts to prostitute women and children across many States. These investigations can lead to local, State, or Federal charges.

To date, the ILNI task forces have rescued more than 2,800 children. Investigations have led to the conviction of more than 1,400 pimps, madams, and their associates who commercially exploit children through prostitution. These convictions have resulted in lengthy sentences, including multiple life sentences and the seizure of real property, vehicles, and monetary assets.

In addition to the ILNI, the FBI also coordinates the Violent Crimes Against Children International Task Force—a select cadre of international law enforcement experts working together to formulate and deliver a dynamic global response to crimes against children through the establishment and furtherance of strategic partnerships, the aggressive engagement of relevant law enforcement, and the extensive use of liaison, operational support, and coordination.

Through this task force we are working closely with our partners to: Reduce the vulnerability of children to acts of sexual exploitation and abuse which are facilitated through the use of computers; identify and rescue child victims; investigate and prosecute sexual predators who use the internet and other on-line services to sexually exploit children for personal or financial gain; and strengthen the capabilities of Federal, State, local, and international law enforcement through training programs and investigative assistance.

Trafficking Exploiting Foreign Nationals

Our CRU investigates trafficking involving foreign nationals, which is often aimed at recent migrants and other economically disadvantaged individuals, particularly women and children. Preying on the vulnerabilities of people seeking a better life, traffickers force migrants without documentation or with precarious immigration status to work in poor, unsafe conditions where they are exploited for prostitution, domestic servitude, migrant farm labor, or toil in restaurants and service industry jobs. Compounding the problem, the number of migrants subjected to these types of crimes is underreported, as many fear deportation or are afraid of retaliation against themselves or their families.

Together with our law enforcement partners at the Department of Homeland Security (DHS), as well as the Department of Labor and the State Department's Diplomatic Security Service, we are working hard to combat trafficking in any form—not only because of the physical and psychological toll it takes on individual victims and their families, but also the profit generated by this exploitation fuels further unlawful migration and organized criminal activity.

Through our efforts, we work with other local, State, Tribal, and Federal law enforcement agencies and National victim-based advocacy groups in joint task forces that combine resources and expertise on the issue. Today, the FBI participates in over 100 human trafficking task forces and working groups around the Nation who work shoulder-to-shoulder in an effort to combat the exploitation of individuals who work in industries, such as agriculture and domestic service, and who are forced into prostitution and/or slave labor.

The FBI's many field offices produce threat assessments to determine the nature and extent of human trafficking in their areas of jurisdiction. They also aggressively pursue human trafficking investigations and develop actionable intelligence. This valuable information aids us with future potential cases, and helps us to better understand the nature and scope of the problem. And finally, these offices are charged with building relationships with civic and community groups and non-Governmental organizations that can refer cases and provide valuable insights and information.

FBI CRU's pending human trafficking investigations have increased from 167 in 2009 to 459 by the end of fiscal year 2012. Since 2009, our investigations in this area have resulted in 480 arrests, 336 informations and indictments, and 258 convictions.

ENFORCEMENT: PROSECUTION

The Department's prosecution efforts are led by two specialized Units, the Civil Rights Division's Human Trafficking Prosecution Unit, and the Criminal Division's Child Exploitation and Obscenity Section, which provide subject-matter expertise and partner with our 94 United States Attorneys' Offices (USAOs) on prosecutions Nation-wide.

The Civil Rights Division, through its Criminal Section Human Trafficking Prosecution Unit (HTPU), in collaboration with USAOs Nation-wide, has principal responsibility for prosecuting forced labor and sex trafficking of adults by force, fraud, and coercion, while CEOS provides expertise in child exploitation crimes, including child sex trafficking, and works in collaboration with USAOs to investigate and prosecute cases arising under Federal statutes prohibiting the commercial sexual exploitation of children and the extraterritorial sexual abuse of children.

Taken together, USAOs, HTPU, and CEOS initiated a total of 128 Federal human trafficking prosecutions in fiscal year 2012, charging 200 defendants. Of these, 162 defendants engaged predominately in sex trafficking and 38 engaged predominantly in labor trafficking, although several defendants engaged in both. In fiscal year 2012, the Civil Rights Division, in coordination with USAOs, initiated 55 prosecutions involving forced labor and sex trafficking of adults by force, fraud, or coercion. Of these, 34 were predominantly sex trafficking and 21 were predominantly labor trafficking; several cases involved both. In fiscal year 2012, CEOS, in coordination with USAOs, initiated 18 prosecutions involving the sex trafficking of children and child sex tourism.

During fiscal year 2012, DOJ convicted a total of 138 traffickers in cases involving forced labor, sex trafficking of adults, and sex trafficking of children. Of these, 105 predominantly involved sex trafficking and 33 predominantly involved labor trafficking, although some cases involved both.

The average prison sentence imposed for Federal trafficking crimes during fiscal year 2012 was 9 years, and terms imposed ranged from probation to life imprisonment. During the reporting period, Federal prosecutors secured life sentences against both sex and labor traffickers in four cases, including a sentence of life plus 20 years, the longest sentence ever imposed in a labor trafficking case.

Civil Rights Division

Since the Department created the HTPU within the Criminal Section of the Civil Rights Division in January 2007, HTPU has played a significant role in coordinating the Department's human trafficking prosecution programs. HTPU's mission is to focus the Civil Rights Division's human trafficking expertise and expand its anti-trafficking enforcement program to increase human trafficking investigations and prosecutions throughout the Nation. HTPU works to enhance DOJ investigation and prosecution of significant human trafficking cases, particularly novel, complex, multi-jurisdictional, and multi-agency cases and those involving transnational organized crime and financial crimes.

Consistent with increases in trafficking caseloads across the Department, in the past 4 fiscal years, from 2009 through 2012, the Civil Rights Division and USAOs have brought 94 labor trafficking cases, compared to 43 such cases over the previous 4 years, an increase of over 118%. This is in addition to the substantial increase in the number of adult sex trafficking cases prosecuted by the Civil Rights Division and USAOs.

The HTPU, the Executive Office for U.S. Attorneys (EOUSA) and multiple USAOs have continued to lead the six anti-trafficking coordination teams (ACTeams) in collaboration with the FBI, DHS, and the Department of Labor. Following a competitive, Nation-wide selection process, six pilot ACTeams were launched in July 2011 in Los Angeles, California; El Paso, Texas; Kansas City, Missouri; Atlanta, Georgia; Miami, Florida; and Memphis, Tennessee. Since that time, the ACTeams, through enhanced coordination among Federal prosecutors and multiple Federal investigative agencies, have developed significant human trafficking investigations and prosecutions, including the first multi-district, multi-defendant combined sex trafficking and forced labor case in the Western District of Texas, the first domestic servitude prosecution in the Western District of Missouri, and the first Eastern European forced labor case initiated in the Northern District of Georgia, in addition to numerous other significant investigations and prosecutions.

Of particular interest to this committee, the Department and DHS have collaborated with Mexican law enforcement counterparts on the U.S./Mexico Human Trafficking Bilateral Enforcement Initiative, which has contributed significantly to restoring the rights and dignity of human trafficking victims through outreach, inter-agency coordination, international collaboration, and capacity building. Through the Initiative, the United States and Mexico have worked as partners to bring high-impact prosecutions under both U.S. and Mexican law to more effectively dismantle human trafficking networks operating across the U.S.-Mexico border, prosecute human traffickers, rescue human trafficking victims, and reunite victims with their families. Significant bilateral cases have been prosecuted in Atlanta, Georgia; Miami, Florida; and New York, New York. To advance the interdisciplinary Initiative, the Department and DHS have participated in meetings in both the United States and Mexico to ensure that simultaneous investigations and prosecutions enhance, rather than impede, each other. These efforts have already resulted in three cross-border collaborative prosecutions, involving defendants who have been sentenced in Mexico and the United States to terms of imprisonment of up to 37.5 years, and resulting in the vindication of the rights of dozens of sex trafficking victims.

Outreach and training continue to be a large part of the Department's efforts to combat human trafficking. HTPU attorneys presented numerous in-person trainings as part of the Federal Law Enforcement Training Center State and Local Law Enforcement Training Symposiums. CRT, FBI, and other Department components joined with the Department of State to create an Advanced Human Trafficking Investigator course at the FBI Training Academy in Quantico, Virginia, for Central American law enforcement officers. The program has trained investigators from El Salvador, Guatemala, Nicaragua, and Panama. DOJ, DHS, and DOL collaborated to develop and deliver the Advanced Human Trafficking Training Program to the ACTeams, bringing Federal agents and Federal prosecutors together for an intensive skill-building and strategic planning to enhance their anti-trafficking enforcement efforts.

Criminal Division

The CEOS' mission is to protect children from sexual exploitation by investigating and prosecuting not only child sex trafficking, but also child pornography, and extraterritorial exploitation of children. CEOS conducts and participates in training for Federal, State, local, and international prosecutors and investigators engaged in efforts to enforce Federal child exploitation laws.

For example, in 2013, CEOS's section chief presented on best practices for investigating and prosecuting child sex trafficking cases at a human trafficking seminar in Riverside, California, and participated in crimes against children training conference hosted by the International Centre for Missing and Exploited Children in Vietnam. Also within the past year, CEOS attorneys presented at international conferences in Taiwan, Mexico, Belgium, and Washington, DC, providing training to law enforcement, prosecutors, State officials, judges, and subject-matter experts from various disciplines in the areas of child sex tourism and trafficking in minors.

In March 2013, Weylin Rodriguez was sentenced to life plus 5 years in prison following his conviction for forcing multiple minor and adult victims to engage in prostitution and for various firearms offenses in the recruitment of three minor females and two young adults to work in prostitution. Rodriguez kidnapped some of his victims, and lured others through false pretenses followed by violence. After luring his victims, he and two co-conspirators (aka his "bottom girls"), advertised the victims for prostitution on-line, and forced the victims to solicit for prostitution on the streets. Rodriguez kept all the money received by the victims for the commercial sex acts. To prevent the victims from leaving his prostitution ring, Rodriguez inflicted severe physical beatings to create an atmosphere of fear. He also threatened the victims with guns on numerous occasions, and shot at a customer in front of a victim. Rodriguez has several prior convictions involving drugs, firearm, as well as a sexual offense against a minor. The case was prosecuted jointly by CEOS and the Middle District of Florida.

In May 2012, James Mozie was sentenced to life imprisonment following his conviction in a jury trial of eight counts of child sex trafficking, one count of conspiracy to commit the same, and one count of production of child pornography. At trial, several juvenile victims testified that they either worked or were recruited to work as prostitutes for Mozie and his girlfriend, Laschell Harris, from their residence in Oakland Park, Florida. When customers arrived at the home, they paid a cover charge to the security guard working the front door. The females, many of them minors, worked in the house dancing for tips and engaging in sexual activity with male customers for money. The seven victims, all minors when the offenses occurred, testified that Mozie required them to have sex with him as part of their "orientation," which he explained was his way of "testing the merchandise." They also testified that Mozie would take sexually explicit pictures of them, which he attached to text messages advertising the brothel. Also in 2012, Harris was sentenced to 156 months imprisonment after pleading guilty to one count of sex trafficking, and co-conspirator Willie Rice, who acted as a security guard for Mozie, was sentenced to 48 months imprisonment after pleading guilty to possessing a handgun while a felon. The case was prosecuted jointly by CEOS and the Southern District of Florida.

Executive Office for United States Attorneys

Consistent with the Consolidated and Further Continuing Appropriations Act, 2012, all USAOs established or participate in human trafficking task forces (HTTF), and collaborate with private partners in several ways. Eighty percent of the HTTFs in which USAOs are involved include members from NGOs. Participating private organizations include community groups, faith-based organizations, victim advocacy groups, academic organizations, medical professionals, and legal aid offices. These private organizations provide various forms of assistance to the HTTFs, including tips on women and girls who were being trafficked, social services for victims, and training in conjunction with USAOs.

PUBLIC AWARENESS, VICTIM SERVICES, AND RESEARCH

Federal Bureau of Investigation

The Department does more than investigate and prosecute those who exploit victims of trafficking. For example, the FBI's Office for Victim Assistance, along with victims specialists from the USAOs and/or other non-Government victim assistance service providers, work with human trafficking victims to advise them of their rights and to ensure they get the help they need to address their short-term and long-term needs—such as legal and repatriation services, immigration relief, housing, employment, education, job training, and child care. Nearly 400 victims have been provided services as a result of Operation Cross Country. With the launch of the Innocence Lost National Initiative, the FBI task forces have encountered significant challenges in identifying and providing services for these victims. Often with histories of poverty, homelessness, and/or exposure to violence and abuse, victims may have difficulties reaching out for help or determining who they can trust. Juveniles who become involved in sexual trafficking face myriad obstacles and enormous needs—including very basic needs such as safe housing, subsistence, and schooling—if they are able to leave that life. In addition, they may need substance abuse treatment, medical treatment for conditions like HIV/AIDS, and mental health services. Many face impediments to reuniting with their family of origin, so they need help to prepare for independent living.

Executive Office for United States Attorneys

In order to prevent and increase the reporting of human trafficking, the Department's Executive Office for United States Attorneys developed a public awareness campaign with the cooperation of Polaris Project, a non-Governmental organization dedicated to combating human trafficking. The campaign's advertisements targeted ethnic groups from countries associated with human trafficking in the United States. An advertisement was developed, translated, and placed in selected newspapers in 18 cities for a period of 2 to 3 months during the fall of 2012. The advertisements defined human trafficking, explained that trafficking violates State and Federal laws, and encouraged readers who considered themselves to be victims of, or witnesses to, human trafficking to call the National Human Trafficking Hotline, which is operated by Polaris with a grant from the Federal Government. Polaris provided statistics that showed a significant increase in calls to the hotline from cities where the ads were placed during the periods of time that the ads were running in those cities.

Office of Justice Programs

In fiscal year 2012, the Department's Bureau of Justice Assistance (BJA) and Office for Victims of Crime (OVC) jointly made awards to seven task force sites to execute a comprehensive approach to combating all forms of trafficking, including sex and labor trafficking of foreign nationals and U.S. citizens (male and female, adults and minors). BJA made seven awards of up to $500,000 for 24 months to support law enforcement agencies (one in each task force site) to coordinate the goals, objectives, and activities of the entire task force in close collaboration with the local USAO and the task force partner victim service organization (one in each task force site) to coordinate the provision of a comprehensive array of culturally and linguistically appropriate services to all trafficking victims identified within the geographic area affected by the task force. OVC made seven awards to victim service provider partners who participate on the task forces. In total, $6,609,586 was awarded by BJA and OVC.

In addition to providing direct services, OVC trafficking victim-service grantees across each grant program work to enhance the community's capacity to identify and respond appropriately to victims of trafficking. From July 1, 2011 to June 30, 2012, grantees trained 28,462 professionals, representing schools and educational institutions, faith-based organizations and religious institutions, victim service providers, civic and business community organizations, and State, Tribal, and local law enforcement. The top five topics covered by grantees were: The definition of human trafficking; identification of human trafficking victims; procedures for reporting human trafficking; services available to victims; and legal assistance for victims of human trafficking.

During fiscal year 2012–2013, OVC represented DOJ by serving as a co-chair along with DHS and the Department of Health and Human Services in the development of the first-ever Federal strategic action plan to strengthen services for trafficking victims. After extensive interagency collaboration, the co-chairs drafted the plan and released it for public comment. Over 300 comments were received and OVC is working to incorporate the public's input. The plan is scheduled for release in January 2014.

In order to ascertain the scope and primary methods of perpetration of human trafficking, identify effective means of prevention, and maximize the impact of available victim services, the National Institute of Justice (NIJ) has maintained the most active research portfolio on trafficking in the United States, making dozens of research awards over the past decade. Recent NIJ awards are tackling the toughest questions asked about human trafficking, including measuring the prevalence of labor trafficking, exploring the perpetration of trafficking and evaluating best practices in service provision. For example, an on-going NIJ-funded project focuses specifically on one of the most under-studied aspects of human trafficking: The relationship between gangs and human trafficking. This project will measure the nature and extent of gang involvement in human trafficking by gathering data from four sources: Victims who are assisted by social service agencies in San Diego County, non-public law enforcement incidence and arrest records, persons identified as trafficking victims and perpetrators at San Diego middle and high schools, and the traffickers themselves.

For fiscal year 2013, NIJ is funding a study focusing on the Somali-American diaspora and its involvement in two transnational crimes: Radicalization to violent extremism and trafficking in persons. This study will build scientific knowledge on these crimes with an emphasis on how transnational issues converge in a context of profound community vulnerability and active criminal networks. The co-occurrence of radicalization and trafficking in disadvantaged refugee and immigrant communities warrants an examination to better understand the transnational and convergence issues involved, and how they can inform evidence-based community practices.

The challenges the Federal Government faces in developing and sustaining effective child welfare and juvenile justice systems and providing effective services to juveniles have been studied and documented at the Department and in other Federal agencies for decades. In April 2013, the Attorney General, acting on a recommendation from the Defending Childhood Task Force, called for the formation of the American Indian and Alaska Native Children Exposed to Violence Task Force (Task Force). In recognition of the unique role the Federal Government plays in Indian Country issues, a working group of Federal agencies was established as part of the Task Force. The working group will complement the objectives of the advisory committee of the Task Force, which will consist of non-Federal experts in children's exposure to violence. The initial focus of the working group will be actions to improve the Federal response to the needs of American Indian and Alaska Native children exposed to violence. This vulnerable population has been identified as being particularly susceptible to being lured by traffickers.

From July 8, 2013 through July 12, 2013, the Department's Office on Violence Against Women (OVW) conducted a site visit to western North Dakota meeting with local law enforcement, Tribal leaders, victim advocates, the U.S. Attorney for North Dakota, State and Tribal coalition leaders, and service providers from both North Dakota and Montana. OVW is exploring providing funds to law enforcement and victim service providers in western North Dakota and eastern Montana to address domestic violence, sexual assault, stalking, and trafficking.

In fiscal year 2012, BJA solicited proposals to address the issue of human trafficking on Tribal lands by developing and providing training to build awareness of the existence of human trafficking in Indian Country, and providing law enforcement and community stakeholders with the tools necessary to begin the process of victim identification, rescue and restoration, while providing appropriate consequences for perpetrators in a consistently applied manner. BJA received four applications through a competitive process and awarded $305,000 to the Upper Midwest Community Policing Institute (UMCPI) to develop and pilot the training.

BJA will design and plan the delivery of Human Trafficking Training to Tribal Law Enforcement which will begin a pilot phase of training by the end of 2013. BJA is planning to seek additional funding to expand the number of sites which can be trained moving forward.

In response to law enforcement concerns about possible human trafficking on the Fort Berthold Reservation in western North Dakota, the U.S. Attorney's Office for the District of North Dakota (USAO–ND), the FBI, and multiple Tribal organizations created a Human Trafficking Working Group to address the abuse of women and children through prostitution on the Fort Berthold Reservation. The work of this group resulted in the April 2012 conviction of a New Town, North Dakota man on 16 counts of sex trafficking, sexual abuse, drug trafficking, and witness tampering. The facts revealed at trial established that the defendant had conspired to distribute marijuana around the Fort Berthold Indian Reservation. As part of this conspiracy, the defendant recruited minors and young adults to be part of a gang. According to testimony at trial, the defendant also used physical force and coercion to cause an adult female he had recruited for the gang to engage in commercial sex acts on the Fort Berthold Indian Reservation and in Williston and Minot. USAO–ND believes that innovative, cooperative efforts, like the investigation that led to this conviction, are essential to battling organized criminal activity on the reservations.

The Department's efforts to combat human trafficking present a multi-faceted approach to a multi-faceted problem. As a result, our efforts span from investigation to prosecution, and are supplemented by an array of investigative, training, outreach, and victim services carried out by a wide range of components. Simply put, we are proud of the work we do in this area, and look forward to continuing to have a leading role in the Government-wide fight against human trafficking.

We thank you again for the opportunity to submit this statement.

Chairman MCCAUL. Members are reminded that additional statements may be submitted for the record.

[The statement of Hon. Gene Green of Texas follows:]

STATEMENT OF HONORABLE GENE GREEN

MARCH 20, 2014

Thank you, Mr. Chairman for holding this hearing today and I would like to welcome our panelists for being here.

Every year, according to the State Department and the Department of Justice, between 14- and 17,000 people are trafficked in the United States.

Due to our status as a border State and our extensive infrastructure, Texas is a major crossroads in the United States for human trafficking and forced labor.

Men, women, and children are subjected to labor trades and sexual violence.

These human beings live in fear; fear of extreme poverty, fear of abuse, and fear of law enforcement.

Many are those without legal status and are terrified to seek help from local, State, and National organizations.

We must work to protect at-risk individuals and create safer neighborhoods and communities in Texas and across the United States.

Living a shadowy existence between violence and deportation is the result of abuse and exploitation by traffickers and a dysfunctional immigration system by the U.S. Government.

Every year, the number of individuals applying for U and T visas increases, therefore we must expand self-petitions and access to visas in an effort to reduce crime and trafficking and offer people a way out of this vicious cycle.

A broken immigration system is the best tool available to a would-be trafficker.

A trafficker can promise jobs, educational opportunities, in short a better life, without fear of reprisal.

Under the threat of harm and punishment, the victims have no recourse.

It has been stated that our system must include prosecution, protection, and prevention.

We, in Congress, must work to shine a light on these criminal practices and enterprises and offer trapped individuals a path towards freedom and salvation.

I thank you for the opportunity to speak and look forward to hearing from our witnesses.

Chairman MCCAUL. We are pleased to have two panels of very distinguished witnesses before us today on this important topic.

Our first witness is Brian Moskowitz, the special agent in charge of Homeland Security Investigations in Houston, Texas, a position he has held since November 2012. In this capacity, Mr. Moskowitz is responsible for investigating efforts under the jurisdiction of the U.S. Immigration and Customs Enforcement in southeast Texas.

Mr. Steven McCraw is the director of the Texas Department of Public Safety, a position he assumed in August 2009. Prior to his service, he served over 20 years in the Federal Bureau of Investigations, at which time I was honored to serve with him in the U.S. Attorney's Office. It is great to have you here today, sir.

Sheriff Adrian Garcia, elected sheriff of Harris County, Texas, in 2008, became an officer with the Houston Police Department in 1980. During his 23-year career with HPD, he investigated violent crimes, developed community policing initiatives, and worked to strengthen the relationship between residents and law enforcement. Thank you, sir, for being here.

Ms. Ann Johnson, prosecutor with the Harris County DA's Office, where she specializes in human trafficking, protecting victims, and prosecuting traffickers. During her time in private practice, she represented citizens with civil, criminal, and juvenile matters, appealed cases to the First and Fourteenth Courts of Appeals and the Texas Supreme Court, including the landmark case of In re: B.W., which created a framework for protecting child victims of exploitations and human trafficking. Thank you for being here today as well.

Last but not least, Chief Charles McClelland was sworn in as chief of the Houston Police Department on April 14, 2010. He served over 35 years at the Houston Police Department, joining the department as a patrol officer in 1977 and rising through the ranks to his current position as chief of police. His management experience has touched virtually every aspect of law enforcement throughout his career with the Houston Police Department. We are very proud to have you here today, sir, as well.

The witnesses' full written statements will appear in the record.

The Chairman now recognizes Mr. Moskowitz for 5 minutes.

STATEMENT OF BRIAN M. MOSKOWITZ, HOUSTON SPECIAL AGENT IN CHARGE, IMMIGRATION AND CUSTOMS ENFORCEMENT, U.S. DEPARTMENT OF HOMELAND SECURITY

Mr. MOSKOWITZ. Good morning, Chairman McCaul, Ranking Member Jackson Lee, and distinguished Members of the Texas delegation. Good morning. It is an honor to be able to represent the Houston office at HSI, which is the investigative arm of ICE, and to do so alongside some of our closest law enforcement partners.

The subject of today's hearing is "Combating Human Trafficking in our Major Cities," and I thank the committee for holding it here in Houston to help shine a light on a problem that thrives in the shadows but is often hidden in plain sight. The reality is that hiding in plain sight is much easier in the midst of a bustling major metropolitan area, especially one that is an international transportation hub with a large and diverse population, only a few hundred miles from the border.

Now, this hearing is about the crime of human trafficking, but I think it is important to note the distinction between this crime and another similar-sounding but very different one, human smuggling. This is especially relevant in light of the news from yesterday. Unfortunately, the public, the media, and even law enforcement often use the terms as synonyms, but under Federal law they are not interchangeable. They are separate Federal crimes with very different elements.

At its core, human trafficking is a crime against a person. It is about the exploitation of that person by another, usually through force, fraud, or coercion in either the commercial sex trade or as some form of labor. True human trafficking cases are often difficult to uncover and even more difficult to prosecute for a variety of reasons.

The crime of human smuggling is a crime against the United States, and it generally involves the illegal movement of people across our borders and/or through the interior of our country. It is one of the most prevalent crimes HSI deals with in our part of Texas, and we have no lack of cases.

HSI has developed a comprehensive investigative strategy to attack human trafficking that involves outreach coordination and coalition building. We conduct outreach and provide training to Federal, State, local, and international partners, as well as to NGO's in the private sector, regarding the identification and investigation of human trafficking. For example, here in Houston, HSI provided human trafficking training to over 2,100 State and local law enforcement officers in order to help them meet the training requirements of the State's trafficking law. We also trained front-line USCIS officers so they could help identify potential trafficking victims in the course of their day-to-day duties.

While human trafficking is a global problem, most incidents that occur in the United States are strictly domestic in nature. However, there still is a large number of cases that involve foreign nationals, and in our area of the country, many of those have a nexus to Mexico.

That is why just 2 weeks ago, I went to Mexico City for a series of meetings with officials from the Mexican Federal Police, the Mexican Attorney General's Office, and a leading Mexican NGO. I called for these meetings to see what more our two countries could do against traffickers exploiting our shared border. These meetings were facilitated by the HSI Attache's Office in Mexico and HSI's global footprint is a huge asset not only in our ability to combat human trafficking, but also in our efforts in fighting the hundreds of other Federal crimes that HSI enforces. There have already been benefits from these meetings, including the sharing of intelligence and suspect information, and I expect to host some of these officials up here in Houston in the future.

Given the scope of the problem, no one country, let alone no one agency, can adequately address this issue on its own. It requires partnerships and coordinated efforts both inside and outside of Government to develop, lead, share information, work jointly on investigations, and provide assistance to victims of all ages.

Last year, I created a dedicated human trafficking group to focus on this issue. Our group is one of the primary law enforcement agency partners in a multi-agency effort coordinated by the U.S. Attorney's Office called the Houston Trafficking and Rescue Alliance, or HTRA. The HTRA consists of over 40 participating agencies and community organizations with investigative training, outreach, and victim service components. Within the HTRA model, HSI special agents primarily focus on trafficking investigations with an international nexus. We also work outside the HTRA with other partner agencies, but we always de-conflict our cases to ensure that we are not duplicating efforts.

Our Houston-based human trafficking group, which currently has 19 open trafficking investigations in the metropolitan area, is focusing its efforts on entities or areas susceptible to exploitation by traffickers, including ethnic massage parlors, cantinas, and domestic workers. We refer cases to either the U.S. Attorney or to the appropriate district attorney's office depending on the facts of the case. For instance, we work many of our spa-related cases with the Harris County District Attorney's Office and ADA Johnson.

While not unique to human trafficking groups, we have over 40 State and local officers, including those from DPS, the Harris County Sheriff's Office, and the Houston Police Department that have cross-designated as Customs Officers under Federal law and embedded within our various investigative groups. These valued task force officers have full access to our resources and information, and their collocation helps facilitate interagency sharing and cooperation and leverages expertise, authorities, and resources.

In addition to the direct efforts of our human trafficking group, I believe that we also impact the trafficking problem by doing the things we normally do in the course of our other investigations. For example, there is little doubt that the significant volume of alien smuggling cases that we investigate has disrupted those who smuggle people for trafficking purposes. The same goes for our worksite enforcement, money laundering, and document and immigration benefit fraud cases. Unfortunately, due to the hidden nature of the crime, we simply may never know or be able to prove the extent of the impact that we have had.

Our approach to human trafficking crimes, as well as others like child exploitation crimes, is victim-centric, and HSI's National Victim Assistance Program is crucial to this effort. Locally our trained victim assistance specialists not only assist victims after the fact, but she is also involved with our agents in pre-operational planning to help anticipate and address the needs of potential victims in advance of their discovery.

Sadly, human trafficking in one form or another has been around for ages. It is a crime about power over others. It is driven by greed and the dark side of the human condition. While I think it is naive to think we can eliminate it, we absolutely can lessen its impact and its reach. We can help educate those who may fall prey to its grasp and bring the full weight of the law down on those who pursue it. We can help rescue those victims we find and encourage others to come forward out of the shadows.

Thank you again for the opportunity to appear before you today. I would be pleased to answer any questions.

[The prepared statement of Mr. Moskowitz follows:]

PREPARED STATEMENT OF BRIAN M. MOSKOWITZ

MARCH 20, 2014

INTRODUCTION

Chairman McCaul, Ranking Member Thompson, and distinguished Members of the committee: Thank you for the opportunity to appear before you today to discuss U.S. Immigration and Customs Enforcement's (ICE's) comprehensive efforts to combat human traffickers who exploit men, women, and children, and to share with you our efforts in this fight against a form of modern-day slavery. I am proud to lead ICE's Homeland Security Investigations (HSI) office here in Houston, which has a significant role in investigating human trafficking crimes and bringing perpetrators of these human rights abuses to justice.

DHS is one of the lead Federal law enforcement agencies responsible for investigating and preventing human trafficking. Our investigative authority, screening authority, and most of our assistance programs are authorized under the Trafficking Victims Protection Act (TVPA) and the subsequent reauthorizations. The men and women of DHS are dedicated to combating the heinous crime of human trafficking using the programs and authorities provided to us by Congress and the President. The Blue Campaign coordinates and unites this work.

The Blue Campaign works with our Federal Government colleagues, foreign governments, international organizations, law enforcement at all levels, non-governmental organizations (NGOs), the faith-based community, the private sector, and the general public to share ideas and resources and build a force-multiplying network of diverse but complementary parts. Partnerships augment our efforts by bringing together diverse experiences, amplifying messages, and leveraging resources. Together, we can effectively combat human trafficking by making sure that people understand the crime, recognize its indicators, and know how to seek help and report tips.

THE GLOBAL SCOPE OF HUMAN TRAFFICKING

Human trafficking takes on countless hidden forms of exploitation. Trafficking is not limited to urban high-crime areas, but is also found in rural agricultural sectors as well as in private homes in affluent neighborhoods. We know that adult men and women are victimized, along with children, and that U.S. citizens are not immune to the actions of traffickers. Traffickers prey on vulnerable populations who have little or no safety net. Men, women, and children are trafficked into forced labor, domestic servitude, and commercial sexual exploitation in the United States and throughout the world. Many of these victims are lured from their homes with false promises of legitimate employment, and then forced or coerced into involuntary servitude, migrant farming, sweatshops, and other exploitative labor in addition to the commercial sex industry.

ICE makes every effort to not only find and rescue victims, but to target and cripple the financial infrastructure and illicit proceeds that allow human trafficking organizations to perpetuate their exploitation. ICE utilizes all of its authorities and resources in a cohesive global enforcement response in order to dismantle the global criminal infrastructure engaged in human trafficking. ICE has developed a comprehensive strategy to combat these criminal organizations through coordination with NGOs and law enforcement, both domestically and abroad, to identify and provide services to trafficking victims and coordinate investigations.

Given the international scope of human trafficking, ICE utilizes its strong international relationships through over 75 offices overseas located in 48 countries to identify and pursue criminal organizations. In order to fully address the transnational scope of these organizations, ICE investigations begin in the source countries where trafficking begins, continues into transit countries, and concludes in the destination countries.

STRATEGIC APPROACH TO COMBATING HUMAN TRAFFICKING

To enhance our investigative capability, target human traffickers globally, and rescue victims, HSI has developed a comprehensive strategy, known as the ICE Trafficking in Persons Strategy (ICE TIPS), which embraces a victim-centered approach. The primary components of this strategy are outreach, coordination, and coalition-building.

- *Outreach*—HSI domestic and attaché offices conduct outreach and provide training to Federal, State, local, and foreign partners, and non-governmental organizations (NGOs) regarding: (1) Victim services, including short-term immigration relief for victims of trafficking; (2) HSI's expertise and role in human trafficking investigations; and (3) ICE's leading role in combating human trafficking. International outreach efforts focus on building awareness and increasing host governments' efforts to combat human trafficking at source and transit countries.
- *Coordination*—No one entity alone can adequately address the problems presented by human trafficking. ICE recognizes that the most effective approach to combating human trafficking involves a collaborative partnership and coordination with law enforcement agencies, NGOs, and private industry. ICE proudly partners with these organizations to develop leads, share information, and work jointly on human trafficking investigations.
- *Coalition Building*—HSI develops and builds on existing partnerships with foreign governments, law enforcement, and NGOs to form long-term strategic relationships that foster collaboration in human trafficking investigations. ICE participates in the Department of Justice (DOJ)-funded Human Trafficking Task Forces (HTTFs) throughout the United States to help unite the investigative abilities of law enforcement with victim services agencies in order to provide a coordinated response during trafficking investigations and victim rescues. The HTTFs ensure that the requirements of law enforcement are balanced against the needs of the victims discovered during the course of investigations.

ADDING TO THESE EFFORTS

HSI helped form a new Federal human trafficking initiative in 2011 called Anti-Trafficking Coordination Teams (ACTeams) as part of a Nation-wide Human Trafficking Enhanced Enforcement Initiative designed to streamline Federal criminal investigations and prosecutions of human trafficking offenses. ACTeams bring together Federal law enforcement personnel from ICE, the DOJ's Federal Bureau of Investigation (FBI), the Department of Labor (DOL) Wage and Hour Division, and DOL's Office of the Inspector General, with Federal prosecutors from United States Attorney's Offices and DOJ to develop significant Federal human trafficking investigations and prosecutions.

THE VICTIMS ASSISTANCE PROGRAM

ICE is fully committed to victim-centered investigations and believes victims can be effective, reliable witnesses for successful prosecutions. The victim's testimony provides strong evidence in a criminal prosecution, and victims must be treated with respect and dignity. HSI's Victim Assistance Program (VAP) provides a critical resource to HSI investigations and the ensuing criminal prosecutions by safeguarding victims' rights and ensuring access to the services to which they are entitled by law, as well as providing the assistance they need so that they can participate actively and fully in the criminal justice system process.

The VAP Victim Assistance Specialists support HSI's approximately 6,500 special agents and train them on victims' rights, immigration relief for foreign national victims, human trafficking, child exploitation, forensic interviewing, and other victim issues. Victim Assistance Specialists also assist victims with resources and service referrals for Federal, State, and local crime victim services, as well as referrals to non-governmental and community-based victim service providers. In addition, these specialists support requests and disbursements of funding for urgent, short-term victim needs. They provide on-site victim assistance and operational planning in complex cases involving large numbers of rescued victims, as well as coordination and assistance in cases in which foreign victims are brought to the United States to testify. In addition to assistance for victims, another service provided by HSI's VAP is the Victim Notification Program and hotline, which provides for those prior victims who register notifications of the release from incarceration or removal of criminal alien offenders.

Along with the Victim Assistance Specialists, VAP has four Forensic Interview Specialists (FIS) to conduct legally defensible, victim-sensitive, fact-finding, forensic interviews, which are developmentally appropriate and take into account the victim's age, language skills, mental health, and learning capacity. The VAP FISs also assist with case coordination, operational planning, and case review both domestically and abroad.

MAKING AN IMPACT

Over the past 5 years, ICE has more than doubled the number of human trafficking investigations initiated world-wide. In fiscal year 2013, ICE opened over 1,000 investigations with a nexus to human trafficking that resulted in over 1,800 criminal arrests, the largest numbers of human trafficking cases and criminal arrests ever recorded.

For example, on February 15, 2011, HSI Detroit initiated an investigation after receiving information from local law enforcement and school authorities indicating that a suspect was trafficking four minor children from Togo for forced labor. The investigation revealed that the suspect had petitioned under his asylum application claiming the children were his own, however, investigators discovered that he was not the true father of the children and that he had supplied fraudulent birth certificates in support of their immigration petition. The children stated that they were forced to work in the house, complete all household duties, and care for the suspect's daily needs; and if these duties were not completed, food was withheld or the children were beaten and punished in various ways. HSI Detroit worked with Child Protective Services to ensure that all of the victims' needs were being met. The children were also referred to the University of Michigan Human Trafficking Clinic, which provided them with legal services and assistance with receiving their T-visas. HSI arrested the suspect on May 3, 2011, for five violations including human trafficking. The suspect later pleaded guilty to the visa fraud, mail fraud, and harboring aliens and was found guilty on four counts of forced labor following a Federal jury trial in the Eastern District of Michigan. On March 25, 2013, he was sentenced to 135 months imprisonment and ordered to pay $134,000 in restitution to the victims.

In January 2012, HSI Sioux Falls, South Dakota, conducted an investigation into the sex trafficking of minor females in the Sioux Falls metro area. HSI agents worked jointly with Federal and local law enforcement partners to identify several individuals with gang ties who were prostituting numerous women, including minors. The investigation revealed that these individuals were involved in other criminal activities including money laundering, narcotics, and weapons smuggling. The investigation identified two minor female victims and one adult female victim who traffickers lured into their control and exploited for commercial sex acts. A successful sting operation led to the rescue of the girls and the arrest of their traffickers. One victim was assaulted repeatedly over the course of 8 months and forced to perform commercial sex acts in South Dakota, Iowa, Wisconsin, and Illinois. As a result of this investigation, four suspects were arrested and charged with Sex Trafficking of Children or by Force, Fraud, or Coercion, in violation of 18 U.S.C. § 1591. The main suspect was found guilty by a jury and sentenced to three life sentences for Sex Trafficking by Force, Fraud, or Coercion, and Sex Trafficking of a Child. He was also sentenced to 20 years for Interstate Transportation for Prostitution. Two of the remaining suspects were found guilty and also sentenced; one to 30 years, and one to 33½ years. The final suspect is still awaiting sentencing.

IMMIGRATION RELIEF FOR FOREIGN VICTIMS OF HUMAN TRAFFICKING

DHS has streamlined its training about immigration relief for victims to increase awareness among law enforcement agencies. These short- and long-term relief options assist law enforcement in stabilizing victims so that the victim can begin to recover and rebuild his or her life. Victims of trafficking who are non-U.S. citizens can receive immigration relief from ICE and U.S. Citizenship and Immigration Services (USCIS). ICE can provide a short-term immigration relief known as "Continued Presence," which assists certified victims of trafficking to remain in the United States temporarily, and USCIS can provide immigration relief through the T (Victims of Human Trafficking) and U (Victims of Criminal Activity) visas. USCIS adjudicates applications for non-immigrant status related to an individual's certification as a victim of a severe form of trafficking. This non-immigrant status provides longer-term forms of relief for trafficking victims.

CONCLUSION

ICE remains committed to utilizing its authorities and resources to combat human trafficking and identify and rescue the victims of this horrific crime. We will build upon the successes of our outreach and victim-centered approach, and share our lessons learned and expertise to expand the global fight against this horrific crime. We will continue to dismantle and disrupt the criminal organizations engaged in human trafficking until we end the threat that human trafficking poses.

Thank you again for the opportunity to appear before you today and for your continued support of ICE and its law enforcement mission. I would be pleased to answer any questions.

Chairman MCCAUL. Thank you, Brian.
The Chairman now recognizes Mr. McCraw for 5 minutes.

STATEMENT OF STEVEN C. MC CRAW, DIRECTOR, TEXAS DEPARTMENT OF PUBLIC SAFETY

Mr. MCCRAW. Mr. Chairman, Congresswoman Jackson Lee, since I am going to submit my written testimony, I am just going to ignore it and talk a little bit about what my friend over here said.

First of all, ICE does a great job. HSI does a very good job, an outstanding job in terms of working, collaborating. We have people assigned to their task force. The same thing with the sheriff. The same thing with the chief. In Houston, we are very proud of the way that the law enforcement community works together seamlessly whether it is attacking gangs or cartels and certainly human trafficking.

I would like to say this, just to start, the point about trafficking versus smuggling. It is increasingly more difficult to tell the difference between the two. When the business model for the smuggler/trafficker is to ransom and rape its victims and hold them hostage for 3 days, for a clear purpose, to get more money out of them, it is hard to say that they are not victims or they are not being exploited. Yet, they came under the guise of being smuggled across, and certainly that was the first leg of it. We are seeing it. Six months ago, we had a trooper come across a house that was full of individuals. One escaped. By the time he went there, they had been kept for 3 days without food and water. There had been two females that had been molested and sexually assaulted. Several had been ransomed back to family members. This happens all the time. So from our standpoint, we consider that a serious crime in the vein of human trafficking.

As it relates to the smuggling piece, just to look in terms of what SAC Moskowitz has talked about is that what we are seeing in Texas right now over the last year—in fact, since 2011—we have seen an increase of 94 percent of illegal aliens coming in that have been arrested. That is a substantial amount. In fact, the number is over 243,000. Disturbingly is that the unaccompanied children— and some of them were rescued yesterday or rescued by ICE this week. There were over 28,000, about a 221 percent increase in un-accompanied children coming into that have been detained, detected in the State of Texas. That is problematic because they are also the most likely to be victimized. We know there is a demand for child sex, one of the most despicable crimes that you can imagine. In fact, the proof that the depravity of man has no limits is the sexual exploitation of children.

We have investigations with ICE. We have it with the FBI and others, with the sheriff's department, with the police department. We can demonstrate that they are illegal aliens being recruited, being lured into our major cities, but not just our major cities, and then converted and forced into, beaten into sex trafficking.

At the same point in time, we are mindful that there is also a constituency out there that is being preyed upon, and the Con-gresswoman made a good point of that, and that happens to be missing and exploited children. In Texas, that is over 440,000 miss-ing children that are minors, up to 17 years old. In the Nation, it is over 440,000 right now that are missing and exploited children. We have seen it in some of the prostitution cases. We have talked to them. We have worked with other agencies—is that they do lure. As soon as they are gone, the Congresswoman talked about within 48 hours they are targets. They do have a way, and they are using social media to attract them. Once they do get them, they are beat-en, starved, raped, tortured into this life.

Crime has changed so much. In fact, it is more transitory. It is transnational. It is certainly more organized, and it is more covert than we have had to deal with in the past. So it is that veil of se-crecy that it operates in that was mentioned earlier.

Of course, how do you detect this? How do you do it? I agree that the approach that ICE has taken and HSI has taken and certainly the district attorney's office here has taken, the enterprise ap-proach, going after the command and control of sex traffickers is an excellent way of doing it. We certainly participate in their task forces.

But you also have to have an opportunity. We have recognized that sometimes the only hope for a child to be rescued from sex trafficking is by an informed and educated patrol officer on the street that comes in contact and through a series of questions is able to detect them and rescue them. For years, we were unable to use the patrol technique in interdiction to identify them.

But we started an interdiction and protection of children's pro-gram and we have trained over 7,000 police officers and troopers State-wide and Nationally. The whole point is that in 2012 we were able to rescue 29 females that were forced into prostitution, and in 2013, 39. The point is it is not just DPS State troopers doing that, but it is the patrol officers. Every patrol officer needs to be involved in the business of human trafficking and recognizing these things.

So it is one of the things that we are doing with our counterparts in terms of looking at it.

But I can tell you this: It is going to take a multidisciplinary approach. It is going to have to be aggressive. Because it is hidden, because you do not see it on statistical accomplishments, you do not see it in the uniform crime reports, this is not an index crime. Human trafficking is not there. It is always under-reported by victims. They do not come forward. They are afraid whether they are here as undocumented aliens or whether they are here and otherwise have been wrapped up in this industry. So it is important that we aggressively pursue this. We are committed to working with our Federal partners and certainly our local professionals in doing so.

With that, I will entertain any questions or pass the mic off to the high sheriff.

[The prepared statement of Mr. McCraw follows:]

PREPARED STATEMENT OF STEVEN C. MCCRAW

MARCH 20, 2014

Chairman McCaul and Members of this committee: Thank you for the opportunity to testify before you today on a matter of utmost importance to the State of Texas and the Nation. Human trafficking is not only a crime; it is evil. And the pervasive sex trafficking of children is proof that the depravity of man has no limits.

Every day sex traffickers entice, deceive, threaten, beat, imprison, rape, and force children and adults into the commercial sex industry, which is the most prevalent form of human trafficking in Texas and the Nation. These despicable criminals use a variety of ways to recruit their victims, including social media. We have discovered that the younger the child is, the greater the profit in this industry, and according to one academic study, on average, female sex trafficking victims are first victimized between 12 to 14 years of age.

Labor trafficking is even more difficult to detect than sex trafficking and exists primarily in our immigrant communities. Its victims include both legal and illegal immigrants, who are often isolated, threatened, beaten, and forced to pay off unending debt.

Human trafficking is hidden under a veil of underreporting. I can tell you how many vehicles were stolen in the cites of Houston, Dallas, and San Antonio; but no one can tell you how many times children were prostituted on the streets of these cities. Under severe duress, these victims seldom report, and when they do, it is not reflected in the Uniform Crime Reporting (UCR) index crime statistics.

As you know well, Mr. Chairman, the citizens of Texas have great compassion for human trafficking victims and great disdain for those who prey upon them. The State Legislature and leadership of Texas have been on the forefront in combatting human trafficking. In 2003, Texas became one of the first States to pass human trafficking legislation. In subsequent sessions, legislation has been passed to assist victims of trafficking and to increase penalties for those who traffic in people, particularly children. In 2013, the Texas Legislature passed legislation that increased penalties for trafficking, increased victim identification and services, and provided resources to better detect and interdict human trafficking in Texas.

The Texas Department of Public Safety (DPS) recently collaborated with local, State, and Federal agencies to produce the *2014 Texas Human Trafficking Assessment* using the collective information and perspectives of several agencies across the State, including the Houston Police Department, Austin Police Department, Texas Office of Attorney General, Texas Department of Criminal Justice, Federal Bureau of Investigation, U.S. Immigration and Customs Enforcement (ICE), U.S. Customs and Border Protection, U.S. Department of Homeland Security, U.S. Department of Justice, U.S. Department of State, Human Smuggling and Trafficking Center, and the National Center for Missing and Exploited Children. This law enforcement-sensitive assessment was provided to the Texas Legislature oversight committees and the State leadership this week, and we have also provided copies to your committee staff. We are currently working to produce an unclassified version of this assessment that can be shared with the public.

In Texas, human trafficking involves the recruitment, harboring, transporting, or procurement of a person for labor or services for the purpose of involuntary servitude, slavery, or forced commercial sex acts.

Developing a comprehensive understanding of human trafficking requires the consideration of multiple related offenses, such as compelling and promotion of prostitution, sexual exploitation, forced labor, human smuggling, and other crimes. The victims are males and females of different ages, nationalities, and socioeconomic classes.

I would like to share with you some of the findings in the *2014 Texas Human Trafficking Assessment*:

- Sex traffickers in Texas target juvenile runaways, illegal aliens, and other vulnerable victims, using force, fraud, or coercion to compel them into the sex trade. Under Texas and Federal law, force, fraud, and coercion are not necessary elements of sex trafficking when minors are involved. Victims are often manipulated by traffickers to remain with them due to their emotional or financial dependency on the trafficker for food, housing, and other needs. Sex trafficking is conducted by single individuals, small groups, organized networks and gangs; and the younger the child victim is, the more profitable.
- Members and associates of multiple gangs have been reported to be involved in sex trafficking operations in Texas. These gangs include Barrio Azteca, Black Gangster Disciples, Bloods, Crips, Mara Salvatrucha, Sureños, and Tango Blast. Gangs and gang members are attracted to the lucrative nature of this activity due to the potential for large and renewable profits while the risk of detection is perceived to be lower than traditional crimes.
- Labor traffickers often recruit, transport, and employ the legal and illegal immigrants they bring into the United States for the purpose of forced labor and indentured servitude. These immigrants originate from various countries around the world. Labor trafficking victims can be exploited in both rural and urban areas in a variety of industries. There is limited reporting regarding labor trafficking in Texas.
- Human smuggling is distinct from human trafficking; however, there is substantial overlap in many cases. In some instances, human smugglers have been hired specifically to transport sex trafficking victims. In many other cases, crimes that initially begin as human smuggling evolve into human trafficking or a related crime; for instance, illegal aliens may voluntarily enter into an agreement with an alien smuggling organization, but are ultimately kidnapped, ransomed, assaulted, or otherwise exploited.
- Mexican cartels facilitate, control, or benefit from nearly all human smuggling activity along the Texas-Mexico border. Alien smuggling organizations are increasingly active in Texas, as reflected in the increasing number of illegal alien apprehensions. In fiscal year 2013, 243,550 illegal alien apprehensions were reported in Texas sectors, a 94 percent increase since fiscal year 2011. This figure includes 28,352 apprehensions of unaccompanied alien children (UAC), a 221 percent increase from fiscal year 2011. UACs are often brought to the United States to be reunited with family members, and they are particularly vulnerable to exploitation.

Human trafficking is multidimensional, and to effectively combat it in our major cities and elsewhere requires a three-pronged approach: First is the collection, centralization, and analysis of timely data; second, is the seamless coordination of efforts across jurisdictions and disciplines; and finally, it requires the execution of proven strategies that are mutually reinforcing.

In 2009, the Texas Legislature established and directed the Texas Human Trafficking Prevention Task Force, chaired by the Texas Attorney General, to make legislative recommendations to address human trafficking prior to each session. As a result, the 82nd and 83rd Texas Legislatures acted upon the task force's recommendations.

In 2013 the task force and the Texas Office of Attorney General produced a human trafficking prevention manual for criminal justice professionals to educate law enforcement officers, prosecutors, parole officers, social workers, and others who may come in contact with victims of trafficking.

In 2009, DPS—working with the Federal Bureau of Investigation's Behavioral Analysis Unit and the National Center for Missing and Exploited Children—developed the Interdiction for the Protection of Children program (IPC) to train patrol officers on the detection, interdiction, and rescue of child victims of sex trafficking and exploitation, and the proper handling of such cases. We have provided IPC training to more than 3,030 officers in Texas and approximately 4,080 officers outside of Texas. We are working with the International Association of Chiefs of Police to expand this training across the country because children are being traded and transported throughout the Nation on a regular basis to meet the high demand for child sex—some at ages too young to imagine. For most of these children, a skilled and well-informed patrol officer is their only hope of being rescued.

Texas State troopers rescued 39 children in 2013, and 29 children in 2012. And remarkably, since 2010, DPS can account for more than 100 IPC-related child recoveries by troopers and police officers.

One of these rescues occurred in 2013, when a Texas State Trooper conducted a traffic stop and identified a child who was reported as missing and disclosed that she had been compelled into prostitution. She provided information about another child victim, which led to the identification and recovery of the second child from the sex industry as well as the arrest of the subjects.

Importantly, IPC training enables Texas State troopers and officers to identify members of child sex associations, such as "Child-Lovers," "Girl-Love," "Boy-Love" and "Online-Pedophile Activism," who support the sexual exploitation of children. The training has resulted in the arrest of suspects carrying child lures, duct tape, lubricants, condoms, and child pornography before they could prey upon a child and then share the horrific video images of their crimes among this vile and deviant subculture.

For example, in one of these cases, a trooper conducted a traffic stop of a van driven by a registered sex offender with a previous conviction of indecency with a child. The driver was in possession of a puppy, several large knives, Hello Kitty shirts, girls' underwear, hairbands, lubricants, rope, duct tape, and child pornography.

Although, the possession and sharing of child pornography does not meet the legal definition of human trafficking, the high demand for these images results in child victims of commercial sex trafficking here and around the world. Texas currently has 80,173 registered sex offenders, of which 60,704—or 72 percent—involve at least one offense with a child victim. There are several ways in which children are recruited into the commercial sex industry—one of which is through the internet. In Texas, the Office of the Attorney General works with the National Center for Missing and Exploited Children and the U.S. Department of Justice as part of a wider network to identify, arrest, and prosecute adults seeking to entice children into sexual relationships and/or into engaging in commercial sex over the internet. Since this initiative began in 2008, this effort has resulted in 351 arrests and 414 convictions related to sex crimes against children.

In Texas, the local, State, and Federal law enforcement community work closely together in each of our major cities to conduct criminal enterprise investigations and prosecutions to target networks, organizations, and gangs engaged in human trafficking, primarily commercial sex.

For example, agents and officers from eight different agencies assigned to the Houston Human Trafficking Task Force investigated an international sex trafficking group that resulted in the arrest and indictment of 14 people operating bars/brothels in the Houston area. In this case, young undocumented Mexican women and girls were forced to perform commercial sex acts through a combination of means, including the use of locked rooms, threats, and beatings.

Local law enforcement agencies in Texas routinely target sex trafficking at sexually-oriented businesses and other locations being used for this purpose. Frequently these initiatives uncover larger conspiracies involving the sex trafficking of children in other cities.

A significant factor of human trafficking in Texas and elsewhere is a porous international border with Mexico, which places hundreds of thousands of people destined for the United States in the hands of ruthless criminal organizations who exploit them on both sides of the Texas/Mexico border. The women and children are particularly vulnerable to being sexually assaulted by members and operatives of these organizations, and by criminal aliens already in the United States. ICE recently announced that they deported 860 criminal alien sex offenders from Texas in fiscal year 2014, of which 27 percent of these foreign sex offenders were convicted of sex crimes against children. ICE deports more than 2,000 of these sex offenders from Texas a year, and we will continue to assist them in any way we can.

We are not able to discern what percentage of the crimes committed by criminal aliens in Texas is related to human trafficking; however, we do know they seek out and commit crimes in our immigrant communities. Between October 2008 and January 2014, 172,157 criminal aliens were arrested and booked into Texas jails for committing 591,500 different non-immigration crimes, including 2,939 homicides, 7,470 sexual assaults, 6,940 robberies, 1,026 kidnappings, 71,527 assaults and 4,044 terroristic threats.

Texas-based gangs' involvement in the transportation of drugs and people provides them access to illegal aliens, who they extort, rape, and compel into prostitution. Just as gangs have learned that prostitution is highly profitable with perceivably low risk, so have other criminal organizations, many now exclusively focused on commercial sex and frequently leveraging social media to minimize detection and maximize profits.

As long as the border with Mexico remains unsecure and the Nation's demand for the sexual exploitation and indentured servitude of people remains high, Texas will suffer the consequences of being a transshipment and destination center for drug and human trafficking. Those consequences include increases in the deaths of illegal aliens in remote areas, increases in felony vehicle pursuits, pseudo police stops, corruption, and home invasions.

The State of Texas has committed substantial resources to assist our Federal law enforcement partners with its vital mission of securing our border with Mexico. This effort is essential to public safety, homeland security, and combatting human trafficking in our major cities and elsewhere. We will continue to proactively address significant threats to the people of Texas with our local and Federal partners rather than react to them. In Texas, there is no greater priority than protecting our children, so we recently established the Texas Crimes Against Children Center (TCACC) in Austin within the Texas Ranger Division at DPS as part of a multidisciplinary approach to identify and rescue child victims of sex trafficking and sexual assault along our highways and in our cities. The TCACC also provides information and resources related to these crimes that result in the incarceration of the vilest criminals in our State who seek to rob the innocence of children—our most precious resource.

Lastly, I would like to say that what you measure matters. Today's Index Crime Rate categories do not reflect many serious crimes, such as the sex trafficking of a child, kidnapping, and extortion which gives the public a distorted view of the crime environment in which they live. Until the sex trafficking of a child and other related crimes are reflected in the Index Crime Rate or until the National Incident Based Reporting System (NIBRS) is fully adopted, these horrific crimes will not receive the visibility and prioritization they warrant. Nevertheless, I can assure you that in Texas, we will continue to work together with our many partners to address these deplorable crimes, pursue the suspects and protect the victims.

Chairman McCAUL. Steve, I thank you for that.

The Chairman now recognizes Sheriff Garcia for 5 minutes.

STATEMENT OF SHERIFF ADRIAN GARCIA, SHERIFF'S OFFICE, HARRIS COUNTY, TEXAS

Mr. GARCIA. Thank you, Mr. Chairman. I welcome this distinguished panel and thank you for your kind attention here.

I am also honored to be allowed to provide some testimony this morning on a subject that I place in the forefront of my crime-fighting efforts. I give special thanks to the Chairman, to the gentlelady from Texas from our community, and all the distinguished panel for your efforts in working with me and others over the years to serve Harris County well.

But I specifically want to work with you to bring a brighter spotlight on human trafficking. I look forward to working with you and others to develop an effective and strategic plan that should include legislative action, Federal resources, public/private partnerships, public education and awareness, and law enforcement. I believe that a comprehensive approach with these elements is what we need in our metropolis to bring this horrible industry, if possible, to an end.

Here in Harris County, I know that our cooperative efforts will serve you as a model for others to follow.

As a long-lived Houstonian, I am grateful for today's discussion on human trafficking because it has been in our midst here in the Houston-Harris County area in some form or another for many years, just as it has been in other parts of the country and in our State.

However, it is hearings such as this that create the opportunity to work on a united front to save victims from slavery regardless of whether the victim is a female or male, regardless if it is internationally- or domestically-driven, regardless of whether the victims are in this country without the proper permission, regardless if the victims are cleaning, repairing, or building our homes and businesses, regardless if the victims are giving manicures or washing dishes at some local establishment, or regardless if they have been forced into sex slavery. This hearing will afford us the opportunity to have a clear discussion on how prevalent human trafficking is affecting our community and what needs to be done to address it.

For example, Harris County's economic capacity attracts newcomers from across the Nation and from around the world. So new faces are not unusual here, but sometimes people who look like willing visitors are really here under duress and in places that we may naturally suspect, as well as in places that we may have never thought to suspect.

Harris County's profile is much different today than it was in 1959 when my parents left Mexico City to make Houston our home. Today we are proud of the title of being considered one of the most internationally diverse cities in America. It is important that a global economy be part of our business profile. Unfortunately, there are enterprising persons who want to exploit our diversity at the cost of human tragedy and use our diversity to hide their evil activities.

With a culture of tolerance and diversity, our airports and Port of Houston provide gateways to and from around the globe. So in Harris County, we speak over 100 languages every day and we come in all colors. We will continue to welcome those who want to make a contribution to our community or visit lawfully, but we most also remember that there are victims amongst us who are here illegally because of lure or force. In either case, they are victims. Because of the sheer size of our population and land mass, young runaways from down the road or three States away may not raise eyebrows when they arrive here looking to blend into our communities. As a result, it is important to recognize that we not only have international victims of human trafficking, but we have victims of human trafficking that are born right here in the USA.

This is why I have said many times that human trafficking can hide in plain sight, as it has been said by the other guests. If the eyes of law enforcement were ever closed to this, they are certainly not now and at least not in Harris County and especially not within the Harris County Sheriff's Office. Through the saturation of our mobile phone app, I watch Harris County. We want people to know that we are watching for human trafficking and other crimes, and we need them to do so as well.

The Harris County Sheriff's Office takes a multi-pronged approach to fighting along this crucial battlefront.

First, we work as an integral part of the Human Trafficking Rescue Alliance, in which our partners, the Houston Police Department, the FBI, and others, work on cases that involve traffickers whose operations cross State and National and international borders. As a former prosecutor, you are well aware of how long and complicated these investigations are, and this is why, in spite of our efforts, the Trafficking Alliance has only been able to prosecute 75 people on charges of human trafficking and related crimes since 2006.

As the sheriff of Harris County, I must state that if we believe that there are more victims and traffickers amongst us, then we must commit more resources and broaden our strategy and not be happy with what we are able to do with what we have available. If there is a victim listening to our testimony, I want them to know that we are trying to find them, help them, and put their pimps in State or Federal prisons. But this does require more resources.

Second, we work in the unincorporated areas of Harris County on the streets, at the hotsheet motels, through websites, working in an undercover capacity to bust prostitutes or customers and their pimps. Prior to my administration in 2008, the Harris County Sheriff's Office only had six deputies dealing with vice issues. All these deputies were males. Today, we have increased that number to 12 to address game rooms and prostitution activities. Of these deputies, 7 are females.

I point this out because for too many years we have been effective at arresting mainly female prostitutes, women who I do not believe grew up with the dream of becoming a prostitute on the streets of Harris County. Rather, they are women or in many cases children who have been exploited for someone else's gain. For that reason, I empowered these female deputies to go after those men who want to buy women like cheap property. I have charged these female deputies with giving those men the taste of the shackles that these women have endured for so many years.

Third, on behalf of those who work with the victims of human trafficking, the Human Trafficking Rescue Alliance has rescued more than 230 victims since its inception, and those victims need resources and support. That is why I applaud groups like Children at Risk led by the hard-hitting Dr. Sanborn; Free the Captives led by a powerful Julie Waters; the Tahirih Justice Center led by dynamic Anne Chandler; Force for Compassion led by the dynamic duo of Jana Rankin and Jackelyn Iloff, and Redeemed Ministries led by the fearless Dennis Mark. These groups are just a few who are stepping up to help and do what they can in this fight. However, these groups are overwhelmed and the victims need shelters, legal counsel, and other resources to help them in their recovery.

Also, I have leveraged technology like our Been Missing website and its mobile app to our efforts to recover runaways and missing persons who have disappeared from our community and who may be under the control of pimps and drug dealers.

I have also increased the knowledge of our staff and our deputies, our professional detention officers on the elements of human trafficking so they can do better at recognizing it.

Although we have made progress, I ask for your help in creating greater awareness of this terrible industry. Whenever the Harris County Sheriff's Office announces the results of an undercover sting operation, there are some people in the community who say that we ought to use our resources more to go after violent criminals. The reality is that this is not a victimless crime, and a lot of people are adversely affected by it.

I got the rest of the testimony, but at the end of the day, there are two things that I need your help with, Members of this distinguished panel.

One, let us support legislation like what Congressman Poe has proposed for justice, for helping the victims of human trafficking.

Second, we got to understand that comprehensive immigration reform is a part of the solution. You know, when my parents decided to come here, they could have turned to a smuggler, but instead, they had an immigration system that worked back in 1959. If not for that system that worked at that time, my fate could have been very different.

Thank you.

[The prepared statement of Mr. Garcia follows:]

PREPARED STATEMENT OF ADRIAN GARCIA

MARCH 20, 2014

Thank you, Members of Congress, for inviting me to testify today about a subject that I have placed at the forefront of my crime-fighting efforts. I give special thanks to you, Chairman McCaul, for working with me over the years—not only to serve Harris County well, but specifically to put a spotlight on human trafficking. I look forward to working with you and others to develop an effective strategic plan that should include legislative action, Federal resources, Public-Private-Partnerships, public education and awareness, and law enforcement. I believe that a comprehensive approach with these elements is what we need in our metropolis to bring this horrible industry to an end. Here in Harris County, I know that our cooperative efforts will serve as a model for others to follow.

As a life-long Houstonian, I am grateful for today's discussion on human trafficking because it has been in our midst here in the Houston/Harris County area in some form or another for many years, just as it has been in other parts of our State and country. However, it is hearings such as this that create the opportunity to work on a united front to save victims from slavery; regardless of whether the victim is a female or male; regardless of it is internationally or domestically driven; regardless of whether the victims are in this country without the proper permission; regardless if the victims are cleaning, repairing, or building our homes or businesses; regardless if the victims are giving manicures or washing dishes at some local establishment; or regardless if they have been forced into sex slavery.

This hearing will afford us the opportunity to have a clear discussion as to how prevalent human trafficking is affecting our community, and what needs to be done to address it.

For example:

- Harris County's economic capacity attracts newcomers from across the Nation and from around the world. So, new faces are not unusual here but sometimes people who look like willing visitors are really here under duress and in places that we may naturally suspect, as well as in places that we have never thought to suspect.
- Harris County's profile is much different today than it was in 1959 when my parents left Mexico City to make Houston our home. Today, we are proud of the title of being considered one of the most internationally diverse cities in America! It is important that a global economy be a part of our business profile, unfortunately there are enterprising persons want to exploit our diversity at the cost of human tragedy, and use our diversity to hide their evil activities.
- With a culture of tolerance and diversity, our airports and the Port of Houston provide gateways to and from around the globe, so in Harris County we speak over a 100 languages every day and we come in all colors. We will continue to welcome those who want to make a contribution to our community or visit lawfully, but we must also remember that there are victims amongst us who are here illegally because of lure or force, in either case, they are victims.
- Because of the sheer size of our population and land mass, young runaways from down the road or three States away may not raise eyebrows when they arrive here looking to blend into our communities. As a result, it is important to recognize that we not only have international victims of human trafficking but we have victims of human trafficking that are born right here in the United States of America.

This is why I have said many times, that human trafficking can hide in plain sight in Harris County. If the eyes of local law enforcement were ever closed to this, they certainly are not now, at least not within the Harris County Sheriff's Office. Through the saturation of our mobile phone app "I Watch Harris County", we want people to know that we are watching for human trafficking and other crimes and we need them to do so as well!

The Harris County Sheriff's Office takes a multi-pronged approach to fighting along this crucial battlefront:

- First, we work as integral part of the Human Trafficking Rescue Alliance, in which our partners are the Houston Police Department and the FBI, and the cases often involve traffickers whose operations cross State or National borders. As a former Federal prosecutor, you are aware how long and complicated these investigations are and that is why, in spite of our efforts, the Human Trafficking Rescue Alliance has only been able to prosecute 75 people on charges of human trafficking and related crimes since 2006.

  As the Sheriff of Harris County I must state that if we believe there are more victims and traffickers amongst us, then we must commit more resources and broaden our strategy, and not be happy with what we are able to do with what we have available. If there is a victim listening to our testimony, I want them to know that we are trying to find them, help them, and put their pimps in State or Federal prison. But this does require more resources.

- Secondly, we work in the unincorporated area of Harris County, in the streets, in the hotsheet motels and through websites, sometimes undercover, to bust prostitutes, their customers, and their pimps. Prior to my administration in 2008, the Harris County Sheriff's Office only had 6 deputies dealing with vice issues; all of these deputies were males. Today, we have increased that number to 12 deputies to address game rooms and prostitution and of these deputies, 7 are females. I point this out because for too many years we have been effective at arresting mainly female prostitutes. Women, who I do not believe grew up with the dream of becoming a prostitute on the streets of Harris County, rather they are women, or in many cases children who have been exploited for someone else's gain. For that reason, I empowered these female deputies to go after those men, who want to buy women like cheap property. I have charged these female deputies with giving those men a feel of the shackles that these women have endured for so many years.

- Thirdly, I advocate on behalf of those who work with the victims of human trafficking. The Human Trafficking Rescue Alliance has rescued more than 230 local victims since its inception, and those victims need resources and support, and that is why I applaud groups like:
  - "Free the Captives" led by powerhouse Julie Waters;
  - "Tahirih (Ta-ha-ray) Justice Center" led by the dynamic, Anne Chandler;
  - "Force for Compassion" led by the dynamic duo of Jana Rankin and Jackelyn Iloff;
  - "Redeemed Ministries" led by the fearless, Dennis Mark.
  - These groups are just a few who are stepping up to help and do what they can in this fight. However, these groups are overwhelmed and the victims need shelters, legal counsel, and other resources to help them in their recovery.

- Also, I have leveraged technology like our "Been Missing" website and its mobile app to our efforts to recover runaways and missing persons who have disappeared from our community, and who may be under the control of pimps or drug dealers.

- I have also increased the knowledge of all my staff, our deputies, and our professional detention officers, on the elements of human trafficking so that we can do better at recognizing it.

Although we have made progress, I ask for your help in creating a greater awareness to this terrible industry. Whenever the Harris County Sheriff's Office announces the results of an undercover "sting" operation against prostitution, some members of the community consider prostitution a victimless crime and urge us to use our resources to stamp out violent crimes, drug trafficking, and thefts. I need your help to remind the public that the there is a common thread that runs through all of these crimes, because rarely does any one of these criminal enterprises stand alone. Each fuels the other and anytime we can disrupt one criminal enterprise, it affects the others.

To those who think prostitution is a victimless crime: Help remind them that it's a greedy industry that thrives on forced labor, drug addiction, and sometimes even illegal imprisonment. Many who have come through the Harris County Jail, arrested as prostitutes, tell us they were turned onto illegal drugs and were then forced into prostitution to finance their addictions. Still others tell us they were trapped in servitude, unable to access food and medicine, or even their choice of clothing.

So we need to remind folks that stopping prostitution stops other crimes, emancipates victims, and fights against human trafficking. This also explains why we give the news media the mug shots of the men and women we arrest. We are trying to deter the next set of customers and suppliers. We are attacking human trafficking at its roots.

In addition, I want to thank the Texas Legislature and Harris County Commissioners Court, because last year we got new regulations against wayward Sexually Oriented Business. Although, SOBs are legal, we can now take them down if they fail to comply with county licensing requirements. Some SOBs engender prostitution, which engenders human trafficking. So the regulations are an important tool for us in this battle.

We even attack human trafficking from inside the Harris County Jail. I have worked hard to empower inmates to share information about crimes they are aware of in the free-world. Sometimes this information leads to the identification or arrest of pimps and smugglers. I have also started an inmate rehabilitation program, called "Been There Done That", in which a team, led by certified recovery coach who knows first-hand the struggles of prostitutes and drug addicts. She provides valuable counseling to inmates serving time for prostitution or related crimes. In group sessions, some of the inmates speak out about having been trafficked and/or sold for the production of child pornography.

This compelling rehab program has received National publicity, and deservedly so. The recidivism rate for graduates of the program is very low.

At the same time, Harris County's juvenile justice system has become more sophisticated in responding to juvenile victims of human trafficking. I have shared a significant amount of Asset Forfeiture dollars with the Harris County Juvenile Probation Department to help their efforts with juveniles they identify as victims of human trafficking within their system.

You would be right to assume that sex slavery is not the only form of human trafficking in Houston. Several times a year in the unincorporated area of Harris County, where 1.7 million people now live, my deputies encounter "stash houses" where people smuggled across the border are held captive by the smugglers, forced to work in hard labor with scant food and bad living conditions, supposedly to pay off smuggling fees.

And so I ask you to carry my message to your colleagues in Congress on at least these two concrete actions that can be taken:

- First, bi-partisan legislation on the framework of the "Justice for Victims of Trafficking Act" proposed by Sen. Cornyn and Congressman Poe, would provide funding for domestic trafficking deterrence and victims' support programs at the Federal level. Among other things, it would also create a new grant program helping States and local governments to develop and implement comprehensive programs to rescue victims and prosecute human traffickers.

  We welcome other categories of grant funding for technology and equipment. But the real need is funding for more "boots on the ground," meaning personnel so that we can have the necessary investigative team for the actual problem that we believe exists. I am confident in saying more officers dedicated to fighting human trafficking in Harris County would mean more arrests of traffickers. Obviously, I believe that major cities with international airports and a port, in a border State, should get special consideration.

- Secondly, I urge Congress to move on passing sensible immigration reform that would give us even more ammunition against sex slavery and human trafficking. Proposed legislation would include more resources to secure our borders. We need an immigration system that supports those who simply want earn an honest living to support their family back home, an effective Guest Worker Program that meets the demand of our economy could be a key element in putting smugglers out of business.

  In fact, it was the "Bracero" Program of the 40's that provided the pathway for me to be here before you, as a proud American, and as your sheriff. My father helped to build the rail lines and worked in the fields of California because he wanted to get married and start a family back home. Because he played by the rules but more importantly, because the entry process was something he could depend on, was why he was able to drive across the International Bridge in Brownsville, and not have to swim across the Rio Grande.

  So grateful was he of the "permission" to be allowed to enter the United States that the first thing he could think to do as he crossed the bridge was to stop and get everyone out of the station wagon. When my older brother asked what was wrong, he instructed everyone to kneel on the side of the road as he led them in prayer, saying in Spanish "Thank you God for the opportunity to come to this great country! We will be good citizens, we will obey the laws, and we will work hard to give back everything that this country will give us! Amen."

Mr. Chairman, please tell your colleagues that if not for an immigration system that worked back then, my father may have turned to a human trafficker and our fate, my fate could have been a very different one. Thank you.

Chairman McCAUL. Thank you, Sheriff.

The Chairman now recognizes Ms. Johnson for 5 minutes.

STATEMENT OF ANN JOHNSON, ASSISTANT DISTRICT ATTOR-NEY, OFFICE OF THE DISTRICT ATTORNEY, HARRIS COUNTY, TEXAS

Ms. JOHNSON. Thank you, Chairman McCaul, Ranking Member Sheila Jackson Lee, this distinguished panel, our local Texas delegation. Thank you very much for being here to visit with us and to hear about our local efforts. I am honored to be here today on behalf of Harris County District Attorney Devon Anderson and to share with you the efforts our office is making in combating human trafficking, to support victims, and to prosecute those exploiters.

My work in human trafficking began, as the Chairman said, in representing B.W., a 13-year-old child CPS runaway who was being prosecuted for prostitution. When the Texas Supreme Court ruled in that child's favor, it created a landmark decision and put us on a path of affirming that Texas law will protect child victims of prostitution and treat them as a victim and not as an offender.

Since, the Texas legislature has given us the affirmative defense for adults who are prosecuted for prostitution but are victims of human trafficking. We do not want to prosecute victims. We want to identify and recover those that need our help.

Implementing these changes is like turning a large ship, and we need your support. A recent juvenile case highlights the type of challenges that we face. Recently a young child was recovered off of the truck agreeing to sex for a fee. She is 15 years old. She is 4 months pregnant with her second child. She is in and out, having prior CPS and abuse history. She has a runaway history. She has a below-average IQ operating in the third- to fourth-grade level. She is also dealing with a significant drug dependency. The challenge for us what to do to help her. The additional challenge is we have identified this child, but the State Department tells us that we identify .4 percent. So for every one of her, there are 200 more that we need your help in recovering.

Once we find them, often they are brought to the juvenile justice system which cannot be the only answer. These children often are in need of a placement that can treat not only the juvenile and child protective type services, and there are few facilities that are equipped to handle these issues. We are in a constant state of searching for appropriate beds for these children in appropriate treatment facilities and need your help.

Today, alternative courts such as the juvenile GIRLS Court and the adult STAR Court represent a new model in using the justice system to do justice, healing wounds, establishing strength and independence, and to ultimately reduce the rate of recidivism and the cost to the public. State statutes create the establishment of these courts, but unfortunately insufficient grants keep limitations on getting them put into place.

In addition to victim recovery, we are doing everything that we can to prosecute pimps and johns. Simply removing the child from the streets without a consequence for the pimp or the john will merely create a vacuum in which they will go out and find another to fill the void. Children do not have to be forced. They may even be willing because they believe this individual loves them, that it is a boyfriend, and they often do not know that the sexual abuse that is happening to them is against the law.

Human trafficking is a rapid-growing industry, a reported $32 billion industry worldwide. Prostitution, while it is the oldest profession—we are not talking about consensual sex. We are talking about human trafficking. This sexual industry of supply and demand where pimps or business owners provide workers, adult or children, for johns for a fee. A recent articled noted that a pimp in a small market makes $31,000 a week, largely cash. Law enforcement must have the resources to "follow the money" which most often is funneled in subverted ways to avoid detection and make things more difficult. Exploiters widely avoid legal traps, but they will brag and advertise on-line. They may not have been hiding because past statistics show we have not been successful in prosecuting.

However, the district attorney's new approach in providing a human trafficking specialist provides 24-hour support for law enforcement, communication among the agencies that you see here, and since this shift in focus, there have been some 230 cases that have been brought together for review, investigation, and prosecution.

We are in a constant need for being able to bring witnesses to appear in court because often these manipulators and exploiters believe that the amount of manipulation, both mental, financial, and physical, the way that they have groomed their stable to keep them in pocket means that they will not show up and testify against them. Sometimes they may be right. If we do not provide support for victims, both children and adults, and to strengthen our court system through that method, then these exploiters do win.

With each successful prosecution, we also hand over rightfully and legally through offense reports and discovery the information about how we are tracking them, and we see, following so, that on the streets, they then become warnings to exploiters about what to avoid to keep detection from law enforcement. That is why as this industry evolves, as we continue to look and to discover and prosecute, the more they look to evade and evolve. Law enforcement must have the tools not only to remain with them but to pass up and to stay ahead.

Human trafficking enterprises are culturally and operationally different. Houston is littered with sexually-oriented businesses, massage parlors, spas that often house an international population, which is even more complex. Laws provide protection to international victims but conveying these concepts at raid scenes against language barriers and years of cultural programming is a significant challenge.

The open line of communication among the people that you see here is helping, and while systematic protocols need to be put in place, the reality is these cases are complex, require urgent responses, and the ability to think within the framework of the law but outside the box to stay ahead.

We need your help and we are grateful for your support.

[The prepared statement of Ms. Johnson follows:]

PREPARED STATEMENT OF ANN JOHNSON

MARCH 20, 2014

Chairman McCaul, Members of the committee—on behalf of Harris County District Attorney Devon Anderson and myself, thank you for the opportunity to appear before you with Special Agent in Charge Moskowitz, Director McCraw, and Sheriff Garcia to discuss what we are doing in Harris County to combat the epidemic of human trafficking. The people you see here today represent the commitment and cooperation of State and Federal law enforcement agencies to not only identify and bring to justice predators who enslave their fellow human beings, but also to implement a new sensitivity to the victims of human trafficking who are often coerced into committing criminal acts and become dependent on their captors.

MY WORK

In February 2013, Harris County District Attorney Mike Anderson hired me to be a human trafficking specialist with an emphasis on working to help victims and prosecute exploiters.

My legal background prepared me for this work. After serving as a briefing attorney for the Fourteenth Court of Appeals, I served as an assistant district attorney with the Harris County District Attorney's Office. When I later went into private practice, local juvenile judges appointed me to represent children charged with criminal offenses.

One of the cases to which I was appointed resulted in a landmark decision from the Texas Supreme Court. In 2007, I was appointed to represent on appeal a 13-year-old child—B.W.—who had been adjudicated delinquent for prostitution. Working with attorney Michael Choyke, we appealed B.W.'s case to the Texas Supreme Court and the Court not only reversed B.W.'s adjudication, but also expressly affirmed that all children under the age of 14 years are unable to legally consent to sex. In short, they are victims of child prostitution, not offenders.[1]

After B.W. was decided, I made many presentations regarding the decision and the practical and legal challenges we face in attempting to assist children like B.W. Juvenile court judges continued to appoint me to represent children in specialty dockets like the Mental Health Court and the Growing Independence and Restoring Lives (GIRLS) Court.

Since returning to the District Attorney's Office in 2013, our office has pursued investigations and prosecutions of more than 200 cases related to human trafficking. We have also worked with law enforcement officers at human trafficking crime scenes and spoken with children and adults charged with (or rescued from) engaging in prostitution. What follows is an overview of what I have learned about human trafficking.

THE NATURE OF THE PROBLEM—OVERVIEW

Human trafficking is the exploitation of another human being by labor or sex. It is a modern-day form of slavery, impacting the most vulnerable among us and affecting every social group, all genders, and all ages.

Human trafficking is the second-fastest growing criminal enterprise and, unfortunately, Houston is a primary hub. Most of the cases filed involve sexual exploitation. The victims are hidden in plain sight along our streets, concealed in massage parlors, spas, cantinas, strip clubs, and other enterprises in our community, or marketed on internet sites.

Human trafficking is not limited to international victims. A majority of the victims are American children who often have mental deficiencies and end up on the streets on the run from abusive homes or unwanted placements. For survival, they

---

[1] *In re B.W.*, 313 S.W.3d 818 (Tex. 2010).

allow themselves to be recruited by pimps who take advantage of the kind of money that can be made by a child in what is known as the "Game."

THE GAME

The Game is prostitution, a cruel lifestyle in which people are manipulated, controlled by drugs and violence, and ultimately trapped in a life of providing sex to anyone for a fee.

The pimp's prostitutes are his or her resources. The pimp may refer to the prostitutes as "hoes," "girls," "workers," and the group as a "stable."

A hierarchy exist in the stable in which the "bottom" girl, who is closest to and ironically has been with the pimp the longest, helps run the Game by setting up dates and teaching the girls how to act. The bottom girl may beat the other girls for the pimp if they get out of line, or she may take the beating from the pimp, which also sends a message to the other girls in the stable.

Prostitutes may come and go in and out of jail, or be traded among pimps. It takes work for a pimp to build up a stable. For example, a pimp may act as a trick in order to steal a girl from another pimp's stable. Because of this danger, prostitutes are instructed to never look a trick in the eyes. In the Game, if you look another pimp in the eyes, you are choosing to go with them. If so, the pimps will work out an arrangement in which the new pimp pays off the old pimp. Of course, the new pimps do not pay from their own pocket; they have the girl work off the debt.

Pimps demand that girls bring in a daily quota by selling themselves, performing various sex acts in exchange for money. The buyers are known as "tricks" or "johns." Agreeing to sex, oral or straight, in exchange for money is a crime. Accordingly, code language fools no one but it seeks to avoid legal traps. A "date" or "trick" meets a "john" or "trick" because she is "working," "is interested in having fun or getting freaky," and is ready to give a "BJ" or "head" for a "donation" or "roses." Because selling or having sex with a child is a greater crime, the child's age is often given as one of legal consent, such as 18.

The business of prostitution is set up on "the track," the local streets where girls walk waiting to be picked up by a date in a car or taken to local hourly rental motels. Johns are also attracted by internet ads or locations of other sexually-oriented businesses.

Women have described being beaten by their pimp to a degree they were barely able to perform, and still have johns go through with the sex act with them despite their obvious physical injuries. Child victims describe telling johns their real age in hopes the johns will not go through with the sex act and help rescue them. However, their hopes are almost always dashed as the johns, including returning johns, go through with the sex act, provide them money, and let them go back to their pimp. In one case, the john requested the "one with braces." Child victims describe using drugs as a means of numbing the abuse.

TEXAS AND NATIONAL RECOGNITION OF PROSTITUTED CHILDREN

Texas studies related to children and prostitution's effect on them reveal some disturbing trends. For example, in 2009, the Texas House Committee on Human Services noted:

"Human trafficking is a modern day form of slavery . . . Texas has 20 percent of the market in the United States, and Houston is currently the world's largest center for human trafficking . . . [T]he vast majority of domestic victims of human trafficking were minors; approximately 70 percent of the children fall into the sex trade . . . Unfortunately, most of these children are criminalized and placed with Child Protective Services with the result that the child does not receive the necessary services and often falls back under the thumb of traffickers."[2]

As early as 1999, publications produced by The National Center for Missing and Exploited Children and the United States Department of Justice pointed out that "prostitution of children is closely tied to life on the streets," that pimps "look for young girls who are lonely or rebellious, with low self-esteem," and they "prey disproportionately on young runaways."[3] Simply stated, once on the streets, children often engage in "survival sex."

In response to Texas' challenges, the Texas Human Trafficking Prevention Task Force was created to study human trafficking. The Task Force found that identi-

[2] *Bill Analysis*, Tex. C.S.H.B. 4009, 81st Leg. (2009).
[3] Eva J. Klain, J.D., *Prostitution of Children and Child Sex Tourism: An Analysis of Domestic and International Responses*, N.C.M.E.C. (April 1999).

fying child victims is difficult due to a lack of general understanding about human trafficking among those that come in contact with children, the failure of child victims to self-identify, contradictory laws and lack of legislation.[4] The Task Force found:

- 11,942 juveniles were arrested as runaways in 2009.
- Children are approached by traffickers within 48 hours of running away.
- The number of victims identified reflects only .4% of the victims in existence. This means that, for every victim we recover, there are 200 more just like them that we have yet to identify.
- The average age of entry into prostitution is 12 years old.

These risk factors and statistics highlight the need for Texas to secure and protect children immediately upon recovery.

THE CHALLENGES TO PROVIDING CARE FOR PROSTITUTED CHILDREN

Texas has two ways to provide services for and taking custody or possession of a child: The Texas Department of Family and Protective Services (Children's Protective Services, hereafter "CPS") may assist victims of abuse or neglect from birth until age 18; and the Juvenile Justice System may assist children engaged in delinquent (criminal) conduct and in conduct indicating a need for supervision for ages 10 to 17.

Although placement for offenders can be in physically restrictive and locked-down facilities, placement for victims of abuse or neglect or children who engage in conduct indicating a need for supervision, such as running away, generally cannot be placed in secure facilities. Thus, another challenging and recurring scenario confronted by State authorities is recovery of a problematic child in the early morning hours when the proper services are not equipped to handle the recovery and continued placement of the child.

THE LIMITATIONS OF THE JUVENILE JUSTICE SYSTEM AND THE SHIFT IN VIEWING PROSTITUTED CHILDREN AS VICTIMS AND NOT OFFENDERS—IN RE B.W.

The case of *In re B.W.* illustrates many of the commonalities of the population and typical challenges of attempting to provide them placement and services.

B.W. was a 13-year-old runaway from the CPS who had been living on the streets for 14 months. On January 11, 2007, at 10:30 a.m. on a Tuesday morning, she was arrested by Houston Police Department officers for agreeing to oral sex for a fee of $20.00. Officers charged her originally as an adult because she lied about her age. Upon discovery that she was only 13 years old, her case was refiled in the juvenile system. At the time, she made an outcry that she had been living with her "32-year-old boyfriend" who was having sex with her. However, the record remains silent as to any investigation into the "32-year-old boyfriend" or any other person who put her in the position of selling herself. A psychological report indicated B.W. was an "emotionally impoverished, discouraged and dependent adolescent" who "exhibited patterns of feeling sad, downhearted, unworthy." [S]he "yearns for acceptance from others, although her hopes appear to be waning rapidly." Reports also indicated that she carried sexually transmitted diseases and was mentally deficient.

B.W.'s case contained some of the common challenges we see with child victims of prostitution. They do not self-identify as victims and may not know what is happening to them is against the law. They often identify or see their pimps as a boyfriend or love interest and will lie in an attempt to avoid recovery by law enforcement.

In deciding B.W.'s case, the Texas Supreme Court recognized for the first time that children do not freely choose a life of prostitution, but instead are manipulated and controlled by their exploiters.[5] Further noting, the Court wrote:

"It is difficult to reconcile the Legislature's recognition of the special vulnerability of children, and its passage of laws for their protection, with an intent to find that children under 14 understand the nature and consequences of their conduct when they agree to commit a sex act for money, or to consider children quasi-criminal offenders guilty of an act that necessarily involves their own sexual exploitation."[6]

The age limitation on juvenile justice prevents it from being the answer. The case of Shaniya Davis, a 5-year-old child in North Carolina, illustrates the impact this offense can have on children of any age. Media reports show haunting surveillance

---

[4] See Texas Human Trafficking Prevention Task Force Report, January 2011, at 12.
[5] See *In re B.W.*, 313 S.W.3d at 826.
[6] Id. at 821–22.

video of that child being carried by a man through a hotel hallway prior to her killing. The man and Shaniya's mother were prosecuted for human trafficking.

THE PRACTICAL LIMITATIONS OF CHILDREN'S PROTECTIVE SERVICES IN PROVIDING CARE FOR PROSTITUTED CHILDREN

In recognizing these children as victims, CPS is the appropriate vehicle to provide care for these children. However, the practical and legal limitations of existing CPS facilities and services make CPS a problematic and unrealistic resource.

Many prostituted children come from abusive homes or have already been taken into custody or care by the State as a victim of another form of abuse. In this respect, they appear to be a population CPS has already been unable to supervise or help. These children are "runners" and take advantage of the inability of CPS to provide secure lock-down placement.

Officers express extreme frustration with recovering a prostituted child from the streets and returning them to a proper CPS placement facility only to have the child leave because agency representatives have no ability to restrain or stop them. Worse, some children do as instructed by their exploiters: They not only run, they encourage additional girls to run with them.

This does not happen in all facilities. Some secure and therapeutic placement facilities are licensed to serve both CPS dependant and Juvenile Justice's delinquent populations. However, a constant need exists for "beds" in these appropriate facilities.

This challenge raises the need for more proper placement facilities with the capacity to triage a child's initial recovery and treat the child's acute medical, mental health, and drug conditions.

IDENTIFYING CHILDREN

Once a child is on the run, it is difficult to ascertain their true identity. Many times, children give a false date of birth and without the ability to verify the information they are released or processed through adult jail systems undetected.

Strategies exist to help mitigate this problem, however. For example, many States do not report CPS runaways to the Center for Missing and Exploited Children. Adding children to this database could assist recovery.

Existing law enforcement protocols allow for the identification of persons by fingerprints out on the streets. If a child is under the jurisdiction of CPS, however, the State does not obtain the child's fingerprints. This policy should change. Collection of these fingerprints would aid recovery of these vulnerable children. If there are concerns about the child's privacy from such a policy, they can be resolved by adopting a policy of purging fingerprint records upon the child's emancipation or 18th birthday.

JUVENILE JUSTICE RESPONSE TO PROVIDING CARE FOR PROSTITUTED CHILDREN—GROWING INDEPENDENCE AND RESTORING LIVES (GIRLS) COURT

As a result of CPS deficiencies and placement challenges, law enforcement officials tend to use any appropriate delinquency charge to place the child in the secure lock-down facilities of juvenile justice.

In July 2011, the 315th Juvenile District Court had before it a child victim of human trafficking, but the child was also a probationer being lawfully prosecuted for an offense of delinquent conduct. Recognizing the need to provide a victim-centered approach for child victims of human trafficking lawfully brought into the Juvenile Justice System, State District Judge Michael Schneider and Associate Judge Angela Ellis created the GIRLS Court.

Everyone had the desire to handle these cases differently, but the team effort necessary to actually make it happen under then-existing circumstances was remarkable. The GIRLS Court would not have been created without the leadership of the judges and the willingness of the Harris County Juvenile Probation Department to consider the issue a priority in the face of budget constraints.

The GIRLS court was created as a collaborative approach drawing upon the support of the judges, probation officials, other Government agencies, non-profit partners, the Public Defender's Office, private practice attorneys, and the District Attorney's Office. Many professionals began giving their time for weekly staffing and monthly review hearings with the participants and staff members, who make themselves available at all hours. In partnership with organizations such as the YMCA International, local community emergency shelters, and the Children's Assessment Center, existing services and specialized programs were created.

Most of the children in GIRLS Court identified as human trafficking victims have been charged with other offenses, such as failure to identify themselves or possession of marijuana. This program diverts them from standard probation into the GIRLS Court, which targets their individualized needs, and places them in facilities for medical, mental health, or drug treatment.

Examples of some of these children are:

- B, a 13-year-old girl recruited out of a local mental health facility by an older teen who had been trafficked and beaten with a wrench and thrown from a car. B recalled heavy drug use and vague memories of men having sex with her.
- L, who was offered a ride home by a male her friend knew. He drove her home for a couple of weeks and flashed money. He then asked her to make money for him and threatened her mother, having looked up where her mother worked to make the threat seem credible, if she refused. He took L to various cities, branded her with his tattoo, and began working her in strip clubs to engage in prostitution.
- P was taken to another country and left with relatives who began prostituting her in cantinas around the age of 8. Once here, her mother and her mother's boyfriend prostituted her in various motels. She was recovered at the age of 14, but her aunts pressured her not to testify against her mother.

Upon successful completion of the program, GIRLS Court records are sealed to prevent the child from carrying the stigma of a criminal adjudication. When age-appropriate transition to adult and independent living is possible, the girls are transferred to other services.

At its creation, the GIRLS Court founders confronted the one child, and questioned whether enough need existed to create an entire court and program for such victims. A shift in juvenile intake process provided the answer. At this time, 190 referrals have been made for acceptance into GIRLS Court. This population breakdown is 57% African American, 26% Hispanic, 16% White, and 1% Asian. The court has only been able to accommodate 34 participants. Of those, 12 have successfully completed, 3 are on runaway status, and 19 remain on treatment schedule in the program.

In addition to the youth participating in the GIRLS Court, the Harris County Juvenile Probation Department has an assigned supervisor that monitors several of the human trafficking cases that present to the Department that are unable to participate in the GIRLS Court program. This supervisor assists these youth by making referrals to needed services like the YMCA International, group and individual counseling, and psycho-educational training about human trafficking. This supervisor currently has a caseload of 74 youth.

GIRLS Court participants speak of wanting to become attorneys or probation officers in order to impact and rescue others like them. Success is when the girls perceive, voluntarily, that they are no longer controlled or supervised by the program but see themselves as part of the solution. GIRLS Court represents a common-sense solution and a collaborative approach with the vision of breaking the cycle of abuse and recidivism.

THE REVOLVING DOOR OF PROSTITUTED ADULTS AND POSSIBLE SOLUTIONS

The Texas Legislature has also taken important steps toward encouraging reform in the area of adult prostitution.

Like many others, my thinking about prostitution shifted with understanding. As a proud native Houstonian, I did not know what human trafficking was, much less know (or want to believe) that our city was a hub for it. Yet, strip clubs, parlors, and gentleman's clubs are commonplace in our city and there is little talk of the probable criminal activity occurring inside.

Prostitution is glamorized with portrayals in movies like *Pretty Woman*. Unlike the appearance of Julia Roberts, these women are rarely "attractive"; instead, they wear the scars of drug use and violent times on the streets.

In response to our wanting to ensure they knew the activity was illegal, recommendations for repeat offenders were increased. State laws allow for the enhancement of misdemeanor charges to felony charges and incarceration in State jail and prison facilities.[7]

The Texas Legislature recently recognized that incarceration of such offenders is costly; the average annual cost to house an offender in "State jail is $15,500" and an annual cost of "$18,538 for State prison."[8] In contrast, prostitution rehabilitation programs are "identified as a viable, cost-effective, rehabilitative alternative to incarceration, at a much lower cost to the taxpayer of only $4,300 per year." The "high recidivism rate among this population signifies incarceration" has not been effective

---

[7] See Texas Penal Code § 43.02.

[8] See 83(R) Texas Legislative Session, Texas Senate Bill 484, Bill Analysis, 2013.

to break the cycle, which "often come from long histories of abuse, neglect, and addiction."[9]

Many examples exist of adult prostitution defendants trapped in the costly revolving door of criminal conduct:

- V is a 58-year-old arrested 40 times, 32 for prostitution, 4 for pimping.
- C is a 48-year-old woman arrested 59 times, 49 for prostitution, the others for drug-related offenses and endangering by "leaving her small infant children."
- M is a 39-year-old with 39 offenses throughout 4 States since the age of 18.

Unfortunately, prior prostitution convictions may hinder these women from believing that they have any alternative. Some even understand that taking a conviction will result in a life-long criminal history for a crime of moral turpitude, yet they are willing to do it for their pimp, either out of fear or perceived love.

Most of these women are stuck in a life they were brought into as children. For example, a 19-year-old described being in the Game since running from CPS at the age of 13. She described in matter-of-fact terms running naked to the door for the mailman at the age of 3, with her father running naked behind her, having sexually assaulted her. In and out of the CPS system and jail, and having been traded or moved from pimp to pimp, she is looking for something better. Today, she has no reliable place to turn to when she walks out of the Harris County Jail.

A program illustrating the type of success possible is the Harris County STAR (Strength Through Addiction Recovery) Court. The collateral success is evident from the work of Kathy Griffin, a graduate of STAR Court and human trafficking survivor tirelessly dedicated to helping other prostituted people accomplish the same. She started *Been There Done That*, a program assisting prostituted people incarcerated in the Harris County Jail, with the support of Sheriff Adrian Garcia. Her ability to empathize speaks to them in a language they understand and opens doors to recovery.

To that end, Texas passed legislation requiring all counties to adopt a program similar to GIRLS Court for juveniles and to create Prostitution Prevention Courts for adults. However, unfunded mandates or insufficient grants often result in either taking funds from another child or program in need or the failure to implement programs for lack of funds. The concern is that such policies will result in a disincentive to "discover" the population in order to avoid the budget problem. Federal assistance for such programs is needed.

HUMAN TRAFFICKING AS AN INTERNATIONAL CRIMINAL ENTERPRISE

Human trafficking business enterprises are set up like layers of an onion. They are extremely organized and attempt to operate in the most untraceable form, on a cash basis. They separate and divide responsibilities and attempt to create distance and plausible deniability, not only within cities, but across the country. We see international girls brought across State lines and rotated among major cities.

A multi-billion-dollar industry, human trafficking as a business enterprise is also hidden in plain view. Concealed larger prostitution operations are found in massage parlors and spas. A typical location might operate within a strip center. You cannot see inside. The windows are blacked out, but a sign flashes "open." The workers, predominately women, are kept inside and surveillance cameras monitor the exterior and interior. Cameras may be monitored off-site allowing others to remotely wipe digital recording and equipment systems as they see raid teams approach.

Workers often do not leave the facility: The business premises often include a kitchen, shower, and a room lined with beds where workers sleep. Workers provide sexual services to whoever walks in the door, 24 hours a day, 7 days a week. A storage area holds workers' suitcases, some still marked with travel tags from recent flights and workers already hold a ticket for their next destination. They describe being recruited by one person on the phone, picked up by another at the airport, and being dropped off at the business. Others stop by to pick up the cash and they describe the management as very smart, warning: "You will not find them." Ledgers and bank records show thousands of dollars in cash being deposited and funneled through multiple accounts throughout the United States or wired abroad.

These women may have a debt to pay or may have been promised a legitimate job, but when they arrive, an outfit, such as suggestive lingerie, is provided and they are instructed that in order to make more money they have to give "extra" services. One woman let us know that she did not want to commit prostitution, but that she lost a legitimate job and a debt holder against her family, out of this country, connected her with the spa to make sure she could keep paying.

---

[9] Id.

These workers often may have lawfully entered the United States on a student or work visa. Some have false identification or no identification. Often they speak no or limited English. Prostitution enterprise raid operations uncovered internet advertisements listing: "4 young Asian Staff to pick from," "all new Asian staff," and "we have NEW GIRLS every week!"

The pressures of being in a criminal enterprise, coupled with cultural pressures, play a role in their not speaking out against their exploiters to law enforcement.

LAW ENFORCEMENT'S CHALLENGES AND THE NEED FOR INCREASED COLLABORATION TO PROSECUTE EXPLOITERS

The Texas Human Trafficking Prevention Task Force recognized Texas must do more to reduce the supply and demand by prosecuting both the pimps and johns who exploit them. For example, in 2009, only 10 people were sitting in prison—State-wide—for having pimped children.

The Harris County District Attorney's Office is answering that call. Today, Mike Anderson's commitment continues with the leadership of Harris County District Attorney Devon Anderson. District Attorney Anderson is in the unique position of being a former prosecutor, a former Judge presiding over the STAR Court, and one of the founding attorneys representing children on GIRLS Court. She has unique sensitivity to the complicated nature of the offenses and their victims, as well as first-hand experience with these Courts.

While Houston is a hub, our problem is not entirely local. We see pimps from other cities bring their girls to Houston, especially for big venue events such as All Star and championship games. Human trafficking crosses State and international lines and increased communication among all governmental agencies is needed.

Our dedicated position allows a central location where both local, State, and Federal prosecutors and law enforcement are able to reach out 24 hours a day with cases for review, investigation, and prosecution. Implementing such an approach is time-consuming and requires training and outreach and additional work by District Attorney Office prosecutors and investigators.

The approach is leading to identification of co-defendants and victims who are passed among pimps or transported from other counties or States. We are also recovering additional evidence resulting in increased prosecutions of johns, pimps, and owners.

While these connections are being made among individuals, systematic protocols are needed to enable better collaboration. An example of this need is the recovery of a 15-year-old child victim who was placed in a non-secure CPS facility and ran because law enforcement was unable to correctly identify the child and was unable to communicate with another county. If proper methods of identification and communication had been in place, officers would have been able to identify that child and know the child was lawfully under supervision by another juvenile justice system. That child would have been taken to a secure juvenile justice facility to hold until the proper county could pick up the child.

Another example involves an international defendant/potential victim and witness in pending court proceedings in Harris County who was subject to a court subpoena to testify against a business owner. Despite communication with one Federal agency, she and another international defendant/potential victim and witness were allowed to leave the country, with one taken to the airport by Federal authorities after a bail bond was posted by a person connected to the prostitution enterprise. Increased communication and collaboration of the multiple interests of local, State, and Federal authorities is critical.

When given an opportunity to prosecute at a State level, Texas has strict statutes against human trafficking, sexual assaults, compelling prostitution, and aggravated promotion of prostitution. High punishment ranges allow juries the flexibility to see that justice is done.[10]

Juries are responsive to these cases. For example, our office prosecuted Mark Anthony Kentish for pimping a 15-year-old child and a jury found him guilty and assessed his punishment at 45 years in prison. This case and investigation started with a routine traffic stop by a new patrol officer, but because he had been trained to spot signs of human trafficking, he handled the case appropriately and recovered the child.

Resources are needed to train law enforcement to better identify whether a challenging suspect is actually a victim. Misidentifying victims as offenders affirms training by exploiters that society will see these girls and women as "nothing more than a whore" who "won't be believed." Removing the person being prostituted with-

---

[10] See Texas Penal Code Chapters 20, 21, 22, and 43.

out any consequence to the pimp simply creates a vacuum in which the pimp will go out and find another human being to fill the void.

We are making progress and using every tool available to send a message that Harris County will no longer tolerate being a hub of this modern-day form of slavery and to let exploiters know there is a significant cost of engaging in this business. However, typical evidentiary challenges exist similar to other criminal enterprises: Exploiters use false identification, burner phones, vanilla prepaid credit cards, or "straw buyers" to subvert identification requirements. There are internet sites for johns in which they anonymously rate and discuss the sexual services.

Training and resources for local, State, and Federal law enforcement officers is critical to identify operational methods and collect evidence for prosecution.

RECOVERY BY LAW ENFORCEMENT AND COLLABORATION OF ALL IN THE CRIMINAL JUSTICE SYSTEM

Irrespective of their location, recovery of these victims by law enforcement means that many of the people we are trying to recover come to our attention as defendants. Criminal laws against prostitution and local and county ordinances against sexually-oriented businesses provide a vehicle for officers to make an arrest or recovery of victims. Last year, some 190 such cases against sexually-oriented businesses have been filed in Harris County. These ordinances and cases also help efforts by County Attorney Vince Ryan and the County Attorney's Office to shut down business enterprises through civil nuisance lawsuits.

The hope is the arrest gives the potential victim an opportunity to be physically removed from enslavement and an opportunity to reach out to law enforcement for help. However, the complicated nature of viewing those recovered as both offender and victim makes this work difficult. For example, a 17-year-old child in Texas legally may be prosecuted in misdemeanor court as an adult yet also be the child victim of a pimp who is compelling prostitution of one under the age of 18 years old. The difference between knowing if someone over 18 years of age is willingly breaking the law and committing prostitution or is being compelled by force or threat is dependent upon the strength and quality of the investigation and the victim's willingness to self-disclose.

Law enforcement knows as well that, upon arrest, pimps or owners attempt to bond out their girls to keep them working or "in pocket" while charges are pending. Additionally, once the right to counsel attaches, communication with the defendant/potential victim is only accomplished with the assistance of counsel. At that point, communication with law enforcement is either aided or hindered. Some defense attorneys play a key role by understanding and advocating the significance of a criminal charge, availability of defenses, services, and certain legal status protections, such as U and T Visas, allowing cooperation. In other instances, however, counsel might be hired by the exploiter.

Significant resources exist to assist victims. Trying to convince someone to cooperate and their not agreeing to do so is like watching a person drown while holding a life preserver. In one circumstance, a defendant was accompanied to court by a "driver" and "translator" who advised the attorney that she wanted to plea guilty. However, when questioned by the judge and a court interpreter, that was not what she wanted. Yet, she remained unwilling to cooperate with law enforcement. The cultural, financial, and other pressures on these girls and women not to cooperate makes it critical that we have the evidence to make the cases without their cooperation, where possible.

RAISING COMMUNITY AWARENESS AND ACTION

Some suggest that the increased awareness of human trafficking as a problem is actually an attempt to prohibit consensual sex. That argument falsely implies that both parties are consenting. The reality is that one party is not consenting when that party is a child, is mentally deficient, or is meeting a financial quota for another in fear of physical abuse or threat of harm to themselves or others. Identifying the distinction is the challenge we all have accepted.

This issue is complex and addressing and combating it requires in-depth investigations and prosecution of exploiters, along with services for the victims. Accomplishing these tasks successfully requires the assistance and cooperation of multiple governmental agencies, non-profits, and our community at large. Increasing awareness of the damage that human trafficking is doing to communities is a key.

Here in Houston, many organizations have joined this fight. Houston Rescue and Restore, Children at Risk, the Catholic Charities, Free the Captives, and YMCA International are among many local organizations that help us raise awareness of the problem, bring compassion to victims, and join us in seeking solutions.

With our continued work with local, State, and Federal law enforcement to protect victims and prosecute exploiters, we will bring these cases to local juries and give them the opportunity to set the standard for our community. We believe strongly that they will not want Houston, Harris County, Texas, to continue as the major hub for human trafficking and that these juries will see that justice is done.

Our work is just beginning, Congressmen, and we need your help.

Chairman MCCAUL. Thank you, Ms. Johnson. You are truly doing the Lord's work, and we appreciate that.

The Chairman now recognizes Chief McClelland for 5 minutes.

STATEMENT OF CHARLES A. MC CLELLAND, JR., CHIEF, HOUSTON POLICE DEPARTMENT, HOUSTON, TEXAS

Mr. MCCLELLAND. Thank you very much, Chairman McCaul. Certainly I want to thank the Ranking Member, Congresswoman Sheila Jackson Lee for this important panel and this important topic and allowing me the opportunity to represent the Houston Police Department and what we are doing here.

I will submit my testimony, my written statement as my testimony. But I would like to touch on a few topics related to this issue that I think that are very, very important.

No. 1: What is the size and scope of the problem here in Houston in Texas?

No. 2: Why is Houston an attractive hub for human trafficking?

No. 3: What are we doing here in the Houston Police Department in Houston to address this issue?

A couple of success stories and how can the Federal Government help.

According to the National Human Trafficking Resource Center, Texas is the No. 2 State, behind California, when it comes to reported cases and allegations of human trafficking. Houston is the No. 1 city for those reports. Houston is the largest city in Texas. It has close proximity to Mexico. It has a large airport, international airport, large seaport, international seaport. The I–10 corridor stretches from the West Coast of the United States to the East Coast. U.S. 59 stretches from Mexico to Canada. It has a large population of runaways. It is a diverse community. We have a robust economy that is attractive for labor and also a large sex industry. Those are some of the reasons why Houston is a hub and very, very attractive for human traffickers.

What are we doing here in Houston? Well, several things. The Houston Police Department has dedicated an entire unit that started March 1. It is dedicated to human trafficking only. Now, the Vice Division has always addressed human trafficking and those that are being exploited in the sex industry. Every Houston police officer is being trained to recognize and investigate incidents of human trafficking here in this city. We have members of the Houston Police Department on Federal, State, and local task forces, liaisons to the U.S. Attorney's Office, liaisons to the Harris County District Attorney's Office. We have their cooperation and certainly we liaison with all of the nonprofit groups that assist us in rescuing these victims of human trafficking.

To educate the public. The city of Houston started a website, Shine a Light on Houston, to educate just individuals in the community, signs and evidence of human trafficking and how to report that to law enforcement.

Now, a couple of success stories that I would like to talk about that tell you the depth of this problem and also like some of the challenges for law enforcement.

There is a city about 100 miles south of Houston several months ago that needed some investigative work on massage parlors. They did not have the resources and they asked for assistance from the Houston Police Department. After an extensive investigation, we discovered that many of these massage parlors were located in small municipalities just south of Houston. It was young female Chinese nationals that were being exploited, being trafficked, and the proceeds were coming back to Houston to multiple banks here in this city. We were able to intervene, rescue those victims, and break up that operation. But my point to that story is it crosses all jurisdictional lines, boundaries, State lines, and internationally.

The second case I would like to talk about is an 18-year-old that was rescued by the Vice Division. She was being exploited and trafficked in hotels around this city and came to the city from another city out of State. She was stabbed and raped by her john. Although her injuries were not life-threatening, but she certainly needed medical attention, but her pimp refused to get her medical attention until she had made her nightly quota of the money that he expected her to bring in.

Now, what can the Federal Government do to help us here locally?

No. 1, I think we need a National and regional database of suspects and individuals that are involved in human trafficking. Although we have collaboration and data sharing, we need something that is web-based like the law enforcement on-line system, and I think that the Federal Government should take the lead in that to make sure that individuals who are on these task forces and who are charged every single day to interdict and intervene in these cases have access to information across the country.

No. 2, there are many resources that are available to juveniles that are being trafficked. The average victim starts their life and a victim of human trafficking at the age of 12. Many of the individuals that we rescue and come in contact with sometimes are 18 to 21. There are very little resources to support adults in that age range. Most of the resources and nonprofits certainly have more resources geared toward juveniles. So that is something that is a gap in our system that needs to be tightened up.

Last, I would urge all of you to support and pass legislation proposed by Senator Cornyn and Congressman Ted Poe, the Justice for Victims of Trafficking Act. It is very, very important that we do that so we can have seamless enforcement across the country.

Thank you very much.

[The prepared statement of Mr. McClelland follows:]

PREPARED STATEMENT OF CHARLES A. MCCLELLAND, JR.

MARCH 20, 2014

Chairman McCaul and Members of the committee, I would like to thank you for the opportunity to appear before you today and discuss this extremely important issue which challenges us all on every level—global, National, State and local.

For several years now, statistics on human trafficking have consistently shown the State of Texas to rank at or near the top of reported incidents to the National Human Trafficking Resource Center (NHTRC). Additionally, the city of Houston is most commonly referred to as a "hub" for human trafficking with reports to the NHTRC Hotline in Houston far exceeding those of any other city in Texas.

There are many factors here in Houston that come together to make this city a "perfect storm" for human trafficking, including but not limited to:

- Major international airport;
- Major international shipping port;
- Largest city in Texas and closest to the Mexican border;
- I–10 corridor which stretches from the East to the West Coasts;
- US–59 corridor which runs from Mexico to Canada;
- Popular location for minors to runaway;
- Large sex industry with limited regulations;
- Constantly expanding population creating a constant need for labor.

In order to help combat this scourge on our community, I recently authorized the formation of the Houston Police Department's Human Trafficking Unit (HTU) within the Vice Division. The formation of the HTU was intended to consolidate the Department's resources into a single unit for better tracking, quicker response, and more thorough, focused investigations involving human trafficking. In addition to the HTU personnel working within the Vice Division, this new unit also consists of:

- 2 officers assigned to the Houston Innocence Lost Task Force (HILTF) which investigates domestic human trafficking cases, and
- 2 officers assigned to the Harris County Human Trafficking Task Force (HTTF) which investigates international human trafficking cases.

Additionally, the HTU is currently in discussions with U.S. Department of Homeland Security's (ICE) Human Trafficking Unit to share resources and data. HPD's efforts to combat human trafficking are NOT just limited to the formation of the new HTU. The entire Vice Division, which is made up of over 65 Classified and civilian personnel has been reorganized to focus on investigating and combatting human trafficking. On a broader scale, all HPD Classified officers throughout the Department have, or are currently being trained to identify and investigate human trafficking, both in the sex industry and the labor industry. Finally, the HPD is working diligently to establish and nurture relationships not only with area law enforcement agencies but with rescue and support organizations such as Polaris, the YMCA, Catholic Charities, and the Houston Rescue and Restore Coalition.

For years, the city of Houston has fought countless legal battles with various sexually-oriented businesses in an effort to regulate this industry. Late last year, Mayor Annise Parker, with the aid of the city's legal department took a bold step and entered into a settlement agreement of multiple long-standing lawsuits with several area strip clubs. As part of that settlement agreement, these strip clubs can no longer operate "private" rooms which are well-known to be the locations where various criminal acts including prostitution and narcotics take place, and where under-aged girls are hidden away and victimized. This agreement is still in its infancy and considered controversial by some, but the efforts to force members of the sex industry to take responsibility for helping to eradicate human trafficking on their own properties has, so far, shown many positive results.

The Houston Police Department's dedication to combatting human trafficking can best be illustrated in two very recent cases. The first case involved a request for assistance by a local police agency about 100 miles south of Houston to aid in the investigation of a possible human trafficking ring operating a couple of massage parlors in two separate municipalities. The investigation resulted in the dismantling of an organized group that was trafficking female Chinese nationals for prostitution. The operations were being conducted in these two cities while the money was funneled through multiple banks accounts in Houston. This case serves as a great example of the need for law enforcement to work on a "regional" level to combat human trafficking in their jurisdictions.

The second recent case involved an 18-year-old female victim of human trafficking who contacted the NHTRC hotline asking for help to escape her violent pimp. The young victim had been forced to have sex with a "john" who ended up stabbing her and leaving without paying her any money. While her injuries were not life-threatening, she did require medical attention for her injuries; however, the pimp refused to take her to get medical treatment until she earned him more money to make up for the money that the previous "john" did not pay. Vice HTU personnel received the information from NHTRC personnel, and were able to contact, locate, and rescue the young female, and also arrest the pimp and charge him with felony compelling prostitution. The young victim was reunited with family members that day by Vice HTU. This case serves as a great example of how law enforcement and non-governmental organizations can successfully work together to not only rescue the victims of human trafficking, but to also arrest the perpetrators of this crime and to get them off the street and away from the other victims we know are still out there.

I would like to close my testimony by responding to a question that was posed to me by Congresswoman Sheila Jackson Lee—What can the Feds do to help? I have three responses to this very important question.

First, one of the biggest limitations on the ability of area law enforcement agencies to successfully combat human trafficking in and around Houston is our lack of "data sharing." The persons and/or groups that are committing these crimes are not limited by our jurisdictional boundaries. We (local law enforcement) need the Feds to build a Human Trafficking Regional Database in LEO (Law Enforcement On-Line), accessible only to Vice/HT Task Force personnel to store, share, and search data on all aspects of Houston-area Human Trafficking investigations. LEO is a web-based program that is accessible to Federal, State, and local law enforcement officers and can be "silo-ed" or restricted to only certain law enforcement personnel. This would allow Human Trafficking investigators from all over the Houston area to have immediate access to not only their Department's data, but the data from other area agencies to better coordinate their investigations with each other in a much more effective and efficient manner. The technology to accomplish this is already there, and I am asking for the Feds to take the lead in this matter.

Second, most statistics indicate that the average age of a female when she is first victimized into Human Trafficking is 12 years old. For this fact alone, it is obvious why the majority of Federal investigations/prosecutions of human trafficking involve "minors" (those under 18yoa). However, many of the females that my officers are encountering on the streets, in the massage parlors and strip clubs, and on the internet sites are typically age 18–21. We know from experience that while these young women may be adults now, they have in all likelihood been under the control of a pimp/trafficker for many years. We need to take definitive steps to ensure that this group of "victims" does not fall through the cracks because we are focusing on the minors by ensuring that the laws we pass and the support/assistance we establish is also available to these young women.

Finally, there is proposed legislation in Washington being sponsored by Houston area Congressmen including Senator John Cornyn and Congressman Ted Poe, "Justice for Victims of Trafficking Act." This is very important legislation and is worthy of your consideration and support.

Again, I would like to thank Chairman McCaul and each of the committee Members for coming to Houston to address this very important issue. I thank you for your time, for your efforts and most of all, for your leadership.

Chairman MCCAUL. Thank you, Chief, for that powerful testimony.

The Chairman now recognizes himself for 5 minutes for questions.

I want to first take this opportunity to commend the Houston Police Department, ICE, HSI, a great Federal/local law enforcement operation in shutting down a stash house that held over 100 people in that stash house hostage essentially under very, very horrific conditions. I just want to give this opportunity both to you, Mr. Moskowitz and Chief McClelland, to, if you can, tell us what you can about what happened yesterday.

Mr. MOSKOWITZ. Thank you, Mr. Chairman, and I appreciate your comments and I will be sure to pass on your appreciation to the probably 20 or 30 agents that responded and worked through the night, may still be working hopefully not until they wake up, though, and get some rest.

But this is a case that started for us, for HSI, yesterday afternoon based on the long-standing relationship that our agency has with Chief McClelland's agents and detectives. I will let him talk about what they were doing.

But basically they came to us as part of their investigation after they entered a home that was filled with what they believed to be people unlawfully in the country. We responded and spent all night interviewing, processing the scene. We identified and recovered 115 people from outside the United States, as well as five subjects that are going to be charged in Federal court for a variety of Federal offenses, including hostage taking, unlawful possession of a fire-arm, conspiracy to harbor illegal aliens, and that is happening as we speak. So as I know you were a former assistant U.S. attorney, I would not want to get Mr. Magidson upset with me by talking about——

Chairman McCAUL. Nor do I.

Mr. MOSKOWITZ [continuing]. The criminal investigation that is on-going. So I know you all appreciate that.

But needless to say, at this point, based on a preliminary assessment, this is what I talked about in my statement. This is an alien smuggling organization. This is human smuggling at this point.

Now, does that mean that at some point in the future the people who were smuggled in could wind up as trafficking victims? Absolutely. That possibility always exist, although we may never know it.

But in this case, we have rescued those folks. We are processing them. They are given an opportunity to seek guidance and help and assistance and legal counsel. They will be told about the options under Federal law for relief to potential victims.

Now, again, they are not trafficking victims. They are not eligible at this stage for what we call continued presence, which is something that we give as ICE, or a T visa which is for severe victims of trafficking, but this U visa option will be explained to them. Now, I realize there are challenges with that. That is a process that is handled by USCIS, but that is all going on as we speak.

So I am going to turn it over to the Chief.

Chairman McCAUL. Please relay our sincere thanks to your men and women.

Chief.

Mr. McCLELLAND. Well, thank you very much. Certainly I am very, very proud of the men and women of the Houston Police Department who responded to this incident.

Although this is an on-going investigation, the information did come to the Houston Police Department that someone's life was in jeopardy and this was a kidnapping case. In instances such as this, we act immediately on tips or information involving kidnapping, which triggered a coordinated response from the Houston Police Department. Those cases are immediately investigated by the Homicide Division and they coordinate it with the Vice Division, our Criminal Intelligence Division, who do electronic surveillance and other things to support the Vice and Homicide Division. In this particular case, we received credible information and obtained a location where we believed that someone's life was in jeopardy, and we entered a structure under exigent circumstances.

This is the result of what we found, over 100 people stacked on top of each other literally, living in locked-in squalor. The individuals could not get outside of the structure. It had deadbolt locks that was locked from the outside. So they were just being captive as human hostages or slaves.

Although I agree with Brian, this is certainly a smuggling case and many of these individuals could end up in a trafficking situation. But this is a typical smuggling case. There are many times and oftentimes that we get information and tips that lead to the results of finding someone that is being held hostage, normally not

100, but sometimes 2 to 3 to 4 to 5, but the MO is the same. The trafficker or smuggler is paid half the money up front to get the person into the country and the other half of the payment is to take place but the coyote or the smuggler always raises the price.

Chairman MCCAUL. A job well done.

Mr. McCraw, you and I have spent a lot of time at the border. I know last time the Rio Grande sector. Down there I saw the smuggling of illegals across the border, many children in very horrific conditions. Many of them actually do not make it. They are told Houston is that way, and they have no guidance and they die in the desert.

I understand there is a difference between smuggling and trafficking, but I thought your testimony was powerful in terms of there is not always a clear-line distinction. Sometimes the lines are blurred and what may start out as smuggling, as the Chief mentioned, can evolve into a trafficking situation where they are exploited for labor and, unfortunately, for sex. Could you comment on that?

Mr. MCCRAW. Yes. We do not really care. At the end of the day, they are victims.

I will agree that there are some prearranged agreements, and the coyotes will follow through. It is a quid pro quo business. It is a clear smuggling event. The challenge you have, especially when you have unaccompanied children or children they are moving forward, they may be a part of an overt conspiracy to move them into sex slavery. So you do not know. When they are being smuggled, you do not know what the ultimate goal is in terms of them coming in.

But I will say this. Any time when the business model of the smuggler is to hold them hostage—literally hostage, as the chief said—and ransom them back to family members, threaten them with cutting off parts and so forth and so on, and then either beating and, on many occasions, sexually assaulting the females that they are holding in place, is that smuggling or is that trafficking? Whatever it is is wrong, and certainly they are victims and they ought to have the same rights as any victims in those situations. It is important to prosecute to the fullest extent possible those individuals that were involved in that smuggling/trafficking aspect.

Chairman MCCAUL. I could not agree with you more. I think part of the exercise here is to determine what can we at the Federal level do to help. Chief McClelland, you outlined a couple of excellent points.

Agent Moskowitz, what can we do to help you in your efforts?

Mr. MOSKOWITZ. I mean, I think the most important aspect of this crime for us really centers around that victim and the education and awareness of this crime. I think the reason you are seeing a lot more attention to this is because our collective agencies and departments have done a good job of educating the public that this is a problem, and the more you look, the more you find. But working here to build awareness through public campaigns—that plays an important role or working overseas with countries where this crime originates in many places, developing awareness down there as to the crime, and than talking about what rights people have are important things. This is really again victim-centric.

I understand what Steve is saying about I do not care, but in our world and the laws that you passed, we are bound by those definitions. So as horrific as some of these things are, if you are chained to a wall and beaten, unless it meets the elements in the laws that you passed, it is not trafficking under the Federal level and our hands are tied. So we need to change the definition.

Chairman MCCAUL. Maybe that is something we need to address. We will take a look at it.

Last, I will just conclude. I know we have a lot of other Members here. The 2017 Super Bowl is coming up. I visited with the New Jersey police on the Super Bowl up there, security measures. Obviously, it attracts a lot of these trafficker types, and I would hope that, in working with you, we can prepare for that to minimize that from happening in the Houston area at that time.

So with that, the Chairman now recognizes the Ranking Member, Ms. Jackson Lee.

Ms. JACKSON LEE. Thank you very much, Mr. Chairman, and thank you to the witnesses for provocative testimony.

I am not sure if I am between outrage and optimism, outrage because of the horridness of human trafficking.

First, let me thank you, all of you, in your respective positions.

But frankly, this was placed at our desks, and I believe that this is an important statement, that there is a journal that says "Slavery Today." Frankly, if I might just share with you, according to the International Labor Organization, United Nations agency, almost 21 million people world-wide are victims of modern-day slavery in the form of forced labor or commercial sexual exploitation, with the majority of these victims being women and girls.

With respect to the United States, the Federal Government believes there are 17,500 persons trafficked into the country, but the numbers are low because they do not know how to account for them.

I think, Chief, if I was correct in hearing your point or Ms. Johnson, the point was that we get less than .4 percent. Is that correct? The State Department says that we get less than .4 percent. So the numbers exponentially are growing.

My optimism is I do believe that we can find a way to end this, and it does include the fine work of ICE and all of you, but it does include resources and education.

So let me try to pose.

As I indicated, I thank the Chairman. I do believe that Homeland Security has a mark in this, and it looks as if we are gleaning some of the ways that we can collaborate on legislation already offered.

So let me pose a question to ICE. Sometimes this multi-billion business is weapons, narcotics, and trafficking. Can you just say how this interweaves with—your responsibility obviously is the internal enforcement when individuals come to do harm here in the United States. How do you see that playing on each other and how should we be looking to separate and to have a concerted effort against breaking up these conglomerates that fund these kinds of illicit activities?

Mr. MOSKOWITZ. I think, first of all, I want to start off by saying that as part of our DNA, as part of our training, as part of what we do every day, the welfare of the victim is paramount. So all our agents, regardless of whether they are investigating international drug smuggling organizations, international weapons smuggling, organized crime, money laundering, they have had exposure and awareness to the concept of victim first. So because ICE and HSI is an entity that enforces hundreds of various Federal laws in some of the areas I just mentioned and many others, by the things we do every day, we are dismantling the organizations that are responsible for these crimes.

So whether an organization today is moving heroin into the United States or sending illicit technology overseas or trafficking in counterfeit parts, we know that criminal organizations are profit-driven and seek the path of least resistance. So an organization, especially in the drug and human smuggling area, could morph over to human trafficking endeavors. So our approach is going after organizations. So if we disrupt them and we make it too difficult in one area, we would expect a shift to an area that they feel is less of a threat to them.

So we need to keep the pressure on, and that is why we work all these programs. We have investigations in all those areas I just mentioned with the hope that it will disrupt the networks and the organizations. The same routes that you use to smuggle people in who are just trying to get here for whatever reason are the same routes that drug couriers use. It is the same routes that traffickers use. It is the same routes that people may be using to bring money into the country or out of the country.

Ms. JACKSON LEE. So you see that they are interrelated. It is a conglomerate that generates and feeds on each other and it helps promote human trafficking if someone is dealing drugs or weapons, et cetera. They can use the monies and build their industry.

Mr. MOSKOWITZ. With respect to the part of human trafficking that is driven by money. We have not really touched on this, but there are aspects of human trafficking that have nothing to do with money. It is about those smaller individual cases of maybe power or control. That is not going to solve that part. But the part that is driven by organizations that are for profit, yes.

Ms. JACKSON LEE. Let me go to Ms. Johnson and Chief. You saw me hold up a slavery journal. I think as I was listening to Mr. Moskowitz and my good friend, Mr. McCraw, there was a coming together. But I think there is some true accuracy that human trafficking, smuggling—they get interrelated. There may be definitions, but they get interrelated.

So let me take it to the next level. We do not like to say that word in the United States, "slavery," but as someone is held and held and held and can only do what their dictator tells them to do or Chinese young women in massage parlors—give me an assessment of that. I do not want to play with words, but we are almost at that category in some instances. The reason is we need to explain the horror of what is going on. Ms. Johnson.

Ms. JOHNSON. I think one of the important things that we have seen in local Texas studies is that even people that were selling drugs, got out of selling drugs and started selling people because when you sell a drug, it is gone. When you sell a person, as long as you do not beat her to a point she cannot perform, she can keep on performing and keep making you money. That is the kind of offenses that we see, whether they are children or adults. They are mentally and emotionally manipulated into a point of believing that they do not have an out. Often they are groomed to believe that when they see an officer, that they should run from them rather to him.

That is the important type of shift that we are trying to have publicly, is to let these victims know that they are probably coming to the attention of these officers in part of a criminal offense, of which they might naturally be seen as a defendant. But they need to know that these officers are being trained to recognize them differently. The law locally and the prosecutors also desperately want to help them out, which is why we want them to reach out to us so that we can help protect them.

These spas are set up so that there is a room with just beds, and they stay there——

Ms. JACKSON LEE. There is no end.

Ms. JOHNSON [continuing].Twenty-four/seven. Whoever knocks on the door who has money, whatever they ask for is what is to be provided. They physically might be able to leave the door, but somehow there is some restriction against them that they cannot get away. Hopefully the officers being there and taking them out can start to be the light at the end of the tunnel if we can have that breakthrough of communicating with them to let them know that they are now in a safe place and that we are here to try to provide them some help. It is an awful big challenge, and we are grateful for your support in it.

Ms. JACKSON LEE. Chief, if you would, let me just accept your challenge and indicate to you that we are going to be drafting that universal DNA—I have a DNA bill that is very important. I think we can also find collaborative effort on the U visa problem where it gets taken away the minute someone says no, and they might be a child and might not comprehend.

I think Ms. Johnson just stated it. You are held. You cannot go. You are being used over and over again. It is almost like slavery.

Mr. MCCLELLAND. Yes, ma'am. Even a more difficult form of human trafficking is individuals who were brought to this country with some type of legal status and they have a passport and they are in domestic servitude-type situations where their passports are taken, they are paid no money, and the people that exploited them and brought them to this country physically abuse them, sexually abuse them until somehow they finally escape, seek help. But that is a very, very difficult challenge for law enforcement because it is not visible. It is not as visible as those that may work in the sex trade or the adult entertainment industry, but it is still a form of slavery.

Ms. JACKSON LEE. Let me get these last questions. I thank the Chairman very much. Thank you very much, Chief.

Sheriff Garcia, you might want to expand just a little bit on the comprehensive immigration reform, how that would help contain human trafficking.

Mr. McCraw, you have eloquently spoken about it is just a shame about children: 440,000 children, some of whom can be in human trafficking. If you would comment.

I thank both witnesses for their answers.

Mr. GARCIA. Thank you, Congresswoman Lee for your leadership.

In my opinion, there has been a lot of discussion from people who are very, very close to the ground, the activist communities who are speaking on behalf of DREAMers, on behalf of undocumented people in our community that we know exist here.

One of the prevailing things that I continue to hear is that folks under-report crime precisely because there is a prevailing discussion that law enforcement wants to find you if you are undocumented, not because you are a victim, not because you are a witness to a crime, but because you are undocumented. That hurts our efforts. We are in the law enforcement business and our business is strictly dependent on good information and people who are willing to testify.

As long as that debate continues out there, as long as there is a question as to what is or what is not the focus of law enforcement, there is, in my opinion, the probability that people will try to make a business decision as to whether or not they come forward and make themselves available to law enforcement and what Pandora's box that could open up for them in their circumstance.

So I think that comprehensive immigration reform, sensible immigration reform, whatever it may be, is imperative. The current proposals that are here I think speak to one of the challenges that we have and that is securing the border. There is revenue that would be allotted to help and secure that, but we've got to work many different facets towards the middle.

Then last, I want to also just touch on one thing that I do not think has been said enough, and that is that we are speaking essentially the pressures that we are receiving into our homeland. But let us not forget that some of the folks that are victims to sex slavery and victims to—or runaways, as Director McCraw has talked about, that these folks do not necessarily stay victims within the boundaries of the United States. They could be exported to other parts of the world.

Ms. JACKSON LEE. Mr. McCraw.

Mr. MCCRAW. Yes, ma'am. Well, obviously, you know, all victims are tragic, certainly in the sex industry in particular. Children, obviously, are easier to entice and lure, especially the missing children. Moreover, there is a demand for sex with children. The younger, the more expensive, the more they can charge. That is one of the reasons why they are targeted. That is one of the reasons why social media is being used because the traffickers can range from single actors, some individuals that focus just on sex trafficking, and the gangs have figured out that in the business of trafficking, just like was said by the assistant district attorney, is that this a commodity. It not like you steal a car, you sell some drugs. It repays itself daily. Yet the victim, if you can control that victim, you are at less risk in terms of being arrested.

You know, all of it is a priority, but when you look at it in terms of—from the standpoint of prioritization of what we have to, it is to get to the extent possible—leverage all the resources. It cannot just be investigations. It cannot be just education. It cannot be just patrol. It has to be all the disciplines to be able to do some of these things. Coordination, obviously, and cooperation help in that.

54

I appreciate the opportunity to address this committee today. Thank you, ma'am.

Ms. JACKSON LEE. Thank you, Mr. Chairman.

Chairman MCCAUL. The Chairman now recognizes my good friend, Ted Poe, who has introduced two bills on this issue, both of which I am proud to cosponsor.

Mr. POE. Thank you, Mr. Chairman.

I want to thank all of you all for being here today. We got the best of the best, as far as I am concerned. You know, there is no place better than being in Houston, Harris County, Texas, and I think our law enforcement does the best job Nation-wide. I believe that. I have seen other places, but I have seen you all too. So thank you.

This is a massive issue. Let me try to narrow it down and then get some comments from you. We have three really participants.

We have got the trafficker who is in it for the money. As you have said, Mr. McCraw, and as Ms. Johnson has said, there is more money in it now than ever before, better than drugs for them because the drugs are gone, and the consequences are greater of you selling drugs. The consequences are less if you are this trafficker, whether you are a national or international. We got that person. We want to deal with him. Ms. Johnson, you are taking care of those folks.

Then you have on the other end the victim, and in the middle, you have the demand. I want to address the victim and the demand.

We have a mind-set in this country that we treat prostitutes, especially child prostitutes, as criminals. They are put in the juvenile justice system when they are arrested. The reason? You all do not have any place to take them. There are no beds. I understand from Shared Hope there are 5,000 animal shelters in the Nation. That is great. Nothing wrong with animal shelters. I got one of my Dalmatians from the Dalmatian Rescue. But in their most recent report, they have less than 500 beds for child-trafficked victims in the whole country. So we got to treat these kids as victims of crime and not prostitutes.

I am no psychiatrist, but I did spend a lot of time on the bench and prosecuting the crooks too. But you take that victim and you put them in jail, even though they are not a criminal and we know they are not a criminal, that does not help them down the road. They are already labeled. With all of our openness and records and all, that child is going to have a criminal record, and they are always going to have a criminal record. So we have to work on that end and rescue them first. So, hopefully, we can do that working with you all.

I have seen the victims in Central America. I think in this latest raid, almost all of the people that were brought in yesterday were from Central America. They are not from Mexico. I have been to Peru, South America. In fact, I met a girl, 13, that was trafficked in Peru. Her name was Lily. She gave me this armband so I would not forget her. She was trafficked in her own country, then to Guatemala, Honduras. They have trafficking issues there. Many of those girls show up in the United States. Some of them do not, but many of them do.

Then we have the issue of girls in the United States who are runaways, throwaways, and stolen-away that we have to deal with. But they are all victims of crime, and we have to recognize them.

They are hard victims to work with. These are very difficult people. God bless folks like Dr. Sanborn over there who is trying to help these kids.

But that should be our National focus and mind-set with the community that these are victims of crime. I agree with you, Mr. McCraw. It does not make any difference where they are from. That should not be the first question we are asking them. We should ask what happened to them and try to rescue them.

On the victims, we have to communicate this concept of the U visa, and if we have to fix it and make it better, Sheriff, because as you know, these traffickers and these slave owners will tell these young people I will get you deported if you call the police. They cannot get them deported. In fact, they are the ones who are going to get deported after they go to prison. But they believe it. They do not call. It is a cultural thing. We have to change that so they call the police and then law enforcement works with the Feds and we make sure that they are not going to get deported for reporting a crime of human slavery.

So we need to work on that. Your advice on how we can do that is important to this committee.

But last, I do want some comments from you. Talk about the demand. That is the issue I think. It is an economic issue for the trafficker, but there is a demand. I do not call them "johns." I mean, John, you know, he was a good guy. He is from the Bible. Why do we call them "johns"? We ought to call them child abusers because that is what they are. They are the child abuser. I think the weak link in the law is the child abuser, going after them.

In many jurisdictions, we do not print their names. We just put their initials. Hey, it is time to expose them, and they need to go to prison and they need to be exposed. I think part of their sentence ought to be—talking about backpage. We ought to be putting their photographs on backpage after they are convicted so the world knows who these child abusers are.

But the bill that the Chairman has been gracious to talk about that I have sponsored goes after the demand and gives them equal punishment to the trafficker, but also makes them pay the rent on the courthouse in the sense that these Federal judges can fine them fees that goes into a fund that helps the victims of the crime so they have services that they do not get at this time.

So any input, Sheriff, on just the general dynamics of trying to focus on the demand and then after the trafficker as well?

Mr. GARCIA. Congressman, thank you. You are on point. We would not have this conversation if there was not a demand for the commodity of human bodies in this horrible industry.

You know, part of the strategy that we use is as soon as we do an operation, we post and we share with the media the mug shots of all the people that we are arresting, hoping to prevent the next set of horrific circumstances.

This is why I have been concerned about the fact that when we—as a law enforcement agency, you talk about a runaway. You know, it is not going after a bank robber. It is not going after a drug dealer. It is not going after a human trafficker. But we are dealing with sort of a peripheral issue. I think we have to elevate the severity of what a runaway is and the fact that a runaway gone longer than 24 hours becomes exponentially more at risk of becoming a prostitute, boy or girl, and a drug addict. Either way, they are likely to end up in the same place, either in horrible hands or in a county jail.

So I think we have to really reinvent the challenge that runaways—how they fit into this whole circumstance. I think this will help us address the issue of demand. The faster we can recover these folks that have disappeared out of our communities, the quicker we can take commodities off the streets and make it difficult for people who have that desire.

But all your help in prosecuting them and getting these folks, the buyers, the pimps, the people who are making money off of someone else's tragedy, anything we can do to get them off the streets and in shackles is all the better.

Mr. POE. Lock them up.

Thank you, Mr. Chairman.

Chairman MCCAUL. Thank you. That was very powerful.

The Chairman recognizes Mr. Al Green of Texas.

Mr. AL GREEN of Texas. Thank you, Mr. Chairman. I thank you and the Ranking Member—and I say it sincerely—for hosting this hearing today. It is exceedingly important that the empirical evidence that has been shared by expert witnesses be made available to the public, and I am grateful that you have done this.

I am also grateful that you have a history of working across lines, and while I would like to embellish, I will not because it may not help you for me to say a lot of kind things about you.

[Laughter.]

Mr. AL GREEN of Texas. I do have to thank one other group of folk, the people from the news media. They are indispensable. They really are. We absolutely need the message to get to the masses. There is no better way. I think that we can use all of the other social methodologies by which we could communicate, but it really is good to see it on the evening news, codified in the newspaper. It really is. So I thank you as well.

Sheriff, you talked about the young people who are runaways. I want to just add a human touch to this because the chief has mentioned the runaways as well. But we are talking about 12-year-old babies—12-year-old babies. We are not talking about some person who really understands the consequences of actions. I commend you, Ms. Johnson, Attorney Johnson, for what you have done to help these young babies. These are babies. If one-third of all runaways are lured into sex trafficking within 48 hours, we are talking about a lot of 12-year-old babies.

Now, I want to join my friend Judge Poe. He and I practiced law together for many years. But I just believe that he is eminently correct about the punishment. People who traffic babies have got to go to jail, and they have got to stay there a while, a long time. We cannot allow this to become just another crime because the harm is irreparable. It does not end when you extricate, rescue that child. The scars are there for years and years to come. So we have got to do what we can to make sure that the proper level of punishment is accorded these persons who engage in these dastardly deeds I might add.

I want to mention the article that I read in "The Chronicle," and I am going to mention it from "The Chronicle" so that I do not put Mr. Moskowitz or anybody else who may have briefed in anything other than good standing. But I mention this article because in the article there is this language. It says, "Dozens flooded out into the fresh air and sunlight." This is what happened when they approached. This is what this hearing is all about. We want every person who is being trafficked, every person who is being ensnarled, every person who is in involuntary servitude to get out and into the sunlight. Let us give them that chance.

Then it goes on to say that there is a "keep out" sign above the front door. You talk about hiding in plain sight. This is the supreme, superb, ultimate example of hiding in plain sight. The neighbors said they did not see anything going on, had no suspicions as to this type of activity occurring.

But I want to say this. It was in my Congressional district. It was in my Congressional district. I want to go out there and see this. I want to see what this building looks like. I am going to see what hiding in plain sight looks like in a neighborhood. I take this personally. We have got to do something because these are my people. I do not care how they got here. They are my people now. I am responsible for them now. I am going to defend and protect them now. I want the law to protect them now. The Constitution of the United States of America protects anybody in this country. I want them protected. I am going to do all that I can to help them.

Now to a quick question. As you can see, Judge Poe and I can get carried away here. I think he is the greater preacher, however, to be quite honest.

[Laughter.]

Mr. AL GREEN of Texas. I want you to talk for just a moment, if you would. I know that my time is running out, but just about the T visa. Sheriff, if you would, you have had encounters and you can elaborate, but if there are others who want to chime in. The T visa because I think it is an important aspect of being able to prosecute a case, Ms. Johnson, an important aspect of being able to prosecute. So I will start with the sheriff and welcome anyone else who would like to comment.

Mr. GARCIA. Thank you, Congressman.

The visa issue that I mentioned earlier is a circumstance that is a great resource to help victims of human trafficking or victims who are here undocumented and are a victim of a crime. The challenge, though, is particularly in circumstances like what we saw yesterday. We are processing those folks today. We are talking to them. We are interviewing them, and we are asking the question, you know, will you testify, will you get a witness against your oppressors?

Understanding all the things you have read in that news article about how horrific the circumstances were, 115 people, one toilet, incredible stench in that house, and then who knows, as it has been discussed and mentioned, how aggressive the oppressors are, threatening their lives, maybe have already physically abused them, maybe have already sexually assaulted them several times, maybe have already threatened them by they are going to kill their families back home, they know where they live, cooperate or every-body dies. I mean, that is the real threat that these victims exist under. Then immediately after their rescue, we are asking them, will you testify, will you put this guy in jail?

Knowing or not knowing what is ever between their ears and the experiences that they have lived, the answers oftentimes from these traumatized folks is not likely to be a quick yes, anything I can do, I am ready to testify, put me on the stand, I am there. It is not likely to be that. As a result, there is a high probability that the support of the visa process could be delayed. In some cases, it could be denied. There is a need to improve the process in the event that they say no today or do not answer in the affirmative today, that later on the question mark on whether that visa can be applicable to them can be turned over and facilitated for them.

Mr. AL GREEN of Texas. Thank you.

Because of my time—I am over my time, Mr. Chairman—I will yield back and perhaps in some other way you will be able to respond. But thank you, Mr. Chairman.

Chairman MCCAUL. The Chairman now recognizes Mr. Farenthold.

Mr. FARENTHOLD. Thank you very much, Chairman McCaul.

I am going to avoid getting up on the soapbox because I think some of my colleagues have done a far better job than I could.

But I do want to investigate some of these issues and some of the things that we can do about it, more with some questions.

On this panel, you have actually got several Members of the two committees that probably have the most jurisdiction: Homeland Security and Judiciary. Judge Poe, Ms. Jackson Lee, and I serve on Judiciary. That gives us criminal jurisdiction and immigration jurisdiction.

So, Brian, I want to follow up on what Mr. Green was talking about with the T and U visas. Do we have adequate training for our personnel in briefing the victims on that? Is the problem with these visas a legal problem or is it a training and application problem?

Mr. MOSKOWITZ. First of all, just to stress that both the T and the U visa are administered by DHS, but by USCIS, not my agency ICE.

Mr. FARENTHOLD. You guys are the ones that are bringing them the people that are going to want to take advantage of these. From a Federal level, you and the FBI are probably the big boys in bringing them.

Mr. MOSKOWITZ. Yes, we are probably the primary users of it.

So there is a difference in the T and the U visa. First of all, the T visa. It is for long-term immigration relief, and the victim self-petitions. So it is the victim who comes forward. It does not require a law enforcement certification as opposed to the U visa where a chief or the sheriff has to say, yes, this person is a victim. They are not saying they should get the visa or not, just yes, they are a victim from our standpoint. The person has to comply with reasonable requests of law enforcement to help. If that is granted by USCIS, they get to stay here, a work permit, and access to benefits and such.

The U visa again is very similar. It is for a wider variety of crimes.

The key with the T visa, as the law is written, is you must be a victim of a severe form of trafficking under the definition of the Trafficking Victim Protection Act. So that is the key.

Mr. FARENTHOLD. So we can potentially broaden that definition and it might be helpful.

Mr. MOSKOWITZ. It certainly would be within your discretion.

Mr. FARENTHOLD. All right. So under the U visas, we have heard that part of the problem is you are asked to make that decision whether or not you want to testify. For instance, in this stash house that you all got yesterday, they are probably asking that question today or tomorrow, and that has not given the folks time to get over the emotional scars, much less consult with an attorney or even their consulate officials.

Mr. MOSKOWITZ. Now, if we are talking about people from out of the country, they are through the process, the entire process—I mean, you mentioned training. All of our folks are trained whether it is HSI or ERO. They are trained in this process. Throughout the detention facilities where these people are held are signs and access to free phones where they can——

Mr. FARENTHOLD. But you need some time to deal with it, I guess is the point I was talking about.

I am going to try to stay reasonably within my time, and I have several other questions I want to ask. I will go to Chief McClelland. I will give the sheriff an opportunity to answer as well.

While I was sitting up here, I went on-line to one of the more notorious on-line classified sites and went and looked at some of the adult services. I counted four listings in Corpus Christi in the last 24 hours or with today's date on them and 99 in the Houston area. In finding these criminals and the victims, it does not look like you need to do much more than go on-line. I mean, why aren't we just sending people out? I mean, you have advertised for these services that certainly hint at being illegal. Why can you not just go out, either send an undercover officer out there, or go say, hey, let us look around and find the bedroom full of people being held there? Do you not have the resources to do that? Or is there a legal impediment to doing that?

Mr. MCCLELLAND. Well, yes, one is a resource issue. In other cases, it is an information issue. But certainly the social networking has made it much more challenging for law enforcement to interdict people that are being trafficked in the sex industry. No doubt about that. It is certainly more challenging.

But also culturally as a society, it has been somewhat accepting, and the penalties for the individuals that exploit folks that are trafficking in the sex industry is relatively low because people have looked at it as a victimless crime and they do not understand the violence associated with it. If these were people that were on the news every day for murdering someone, yes, they would be getting felonies and they would be going to jail and prison for long periods of time.

Mr. FARENTHOLD. So who is making the choice of those allocation of resources?

Mr. MCCLELLAND. Well, it is a prioritization with myself, the sheriff——

Mr. FARENTHOLD. Obviously, you want to go after a murderer first, but you hear the tragedies associated with these women and you wonder how many deaths you might be able to prevent. I do not mean to be criticizing your department.

Mr. MCCLELLAND. No, no, no.

Mr. FARENTHOLD. I am trying to find out what we can do to help.

Mr. MCCLELLAND. Well, certainly resources, the database, and a more defined law. I mean, you can hear the confusion here and the close link that you have with smuggling, trafficking, and people going across jurisdictional lines.

Mr. FARENTHOLD. I am already out of time, but if the Chairman will indulge me long enough to get the sheriff's answer to that same question, I would appreciate it.

Mr. GARCIA. Thank you.

The chief is correct. The social media websites in particular and how those respective domains operate—one day the IP addresses are available. The next day they have been turned off. You know, it is challenging. We do need better laws to help address this.

But it also brings me back to the issue of how runaways and missing persons play into that particular side of the equation. We have to do better at maybe making resources available for us to use facial recognition technology much more effectively because they are putting pictures up on the site. Maybe that could be a way to address this.

But there is nothing more than I want to do everything I can to put these folks out of business. That is why I have increased specifically the number of female deputies in my vice operations. I made it a huge priority, looking to do more. I have given $300,000 of my asset forfeitures to the Harris County Juvenile Probation Department so they can start a juvenile human trafficking unit. It is a priority. It is important. We got to step up.

Mr. FARENTHOLD. All right. Thank you very much.

Chairman MCCAUL. I want to thank the witnesses for their valuable testimony and insight to the policymakers and lawmakers to, as you put it so well, put them out of business.

So with that, this panel is dismissed, and the clerk will prepare the witness table for our second panel.

We welcome our second panel to today's hearing and thank you for your participation here today in this important matter.

First, Dr. Robert Sanborn is president and CEO of Children at Risk. Under his leadership, Children at Risk expanded its influence in the realm of child welfare advocacy, including the launch of the Public Policy and Law Center, Children at Risk Institute, and the Center to End Trafficking and Exploitation of Children.

Dr. Reena Isaac is an assistant professor of pediatrics with Baylor College of Medicine, and is a consulting physician at Texas Children's Hospital, Child Protection Program. Dr. Isaac serves as a physician advisor for Houston Rescue and Restore Coalition, whose goal is to eliminate human trafficking by empowering the community to take action to rescue and restore victims.

Ms. Cheryl Briggs is a restored survivor of domestic minor sex trafficking and is the founder of the Mission at Serenity Ranch.

Ms. Briggs also serves as a mentor for the Harris County Juvenile Probation Department, Human Trafficking Diversion Court. In January 2014, Ms. Briggs opened My Daughter's House, a safe house that provides long-term transitional housing for young women who have been rescued from trafficking situations and/or forced participation in the commercialized sex industry. Thank you, Ms. Briggs, so much for being here today and telling your story.

Last but not least, Ms. Kathryn Griffin-Townsend is the founder of We've Been There Done That, a reentry program established with the goal of rehabilitating women who have lived through sex trafficking, prostitution, and associated drug addiction. A former cocaine addict and prostitute, Ms. Griffin-Townsend credits rehabilitation programs with changing her life.

The witnesses' full statements will appear in the record.

The Chairman now recognizes Dr. Sanborn for his testimony.

STATEMENT OF ROBERT SANBORN, ED.D., PRESIDENT AND CEO, CHILDREN AT RISK

Mr. SANBORN. Thank you, Chairman McCaul, and I want to thank all of the Members here for their support of this issue.

I also want to recognize Congressman Poe for the End Sex Trafficking Act and the Justice for Victims Act. Both of them are so important for our fight against trafficking, and certainly, Mr. Chairman, your support for that act.

You know, a lot of people have talked today about why Houston is such a hub for trafficking. I think one of the things that we are not talking about is that for all the reasons that people have talked about, the geographic location and a large city, all of those are true. There are a lot of reasons why I love Houston just like the rest of you. But one of the reasons that we do not talk—one of the things we do not talk about is that in Houston we tend to turn a blind eye towards sexually-oriented businesses. We have over 300 sexually-oriented businesses here in Houston. Less than 20 of those are licensed. Yet, there are more here than in any other city in the Nation. We are turning a blind eye and we are saying boys will be boys in many ways.

It gets back to demand, which you talked about, Congressman Poe. We are not doing the things necessary to make sure that those who engage in these services pay a high price for engaging. We make it very easy for men in our society and certainly men in Houston to be able to go on the internet, to go to backpage.com, which I challenge any of you to do, not on your Congressional computers, though——

[Laughter.]

Mr. SANBORN [continuing]. And find out what is happening on backpage.com. You will see the real pictures of real girls that are being trafficked.

Congressman Farenthold, you talked about seeing this morning 99 in Houston, 3 in Corpus Christi. By the end of the evening, we will have up to 300 here in Houston of those posted, and you will see that many of those are children.

When we talk about trafficking in Texas and across the Nation, many times we are talking about child sex trafficking. At Children at Risk, we work in many areas for children, education and hunger and so forth, but the most heartbreaking area is certainly in the area of child trafficking. Over the last three legislative sessions, we have been able to pass and help in the passage of about 28 bills that have given law enforcement the tools necessary to go after traffickers—law enforcement and prosecutors—starting with allowing the Attorney General to create a State-wide task force. This awareness is very, very important.

A couple years ago, a prominent person in town said, Bob, how are we going to sort of give a knockout punch to trafficking. The answer—I said there are really four steps.

One is we need to create all the awareness that we can. People need to understand that trafficking is a problem. We are beginning to do that. I do not think we are where we need to be because a lot of the information—Hollywood has jumped on it. They really have done a lot, but not all of it is correct. There is more that we need to do around awareness.

The second thing that we need to do is public policy. We need to pass more laws that allow prosecutors and law enforcement to go after traffickers. We are just at the tip of the iceberg on that.

The third is we really need to treat our victims. Congressman Poe, you mentioned there are just too few beds. We have opened up a place recently in Houston. Ms. Briggs has a place that she has opened, and there is a couple that are opening up around the country. We did a lot of research at Children at Risk to create a blueprint for some of these safe houses, but we need to do a lot more to make sure that we have places for our victims.

But then finally, it is going after that demand, which is the thing that we are doing the least about, going after those men that feel like it is perfectly fine to buy young women or young girls. These are the things that we can do. We actually have here—this is a crime against humanity, and this is a crime against humanity in our own town, perpetuated by our next-door neighbors. I think we forget to realize that, that this is something happening with the guy next door. We are not doing enough for these johns, these people purchasing these victims to pay the high price.

The good news is that we are fighting in Texas. We are fighting to end trafficking. We are passing as much legislation as we can.

The bad news is that this is a crime driven by this male population, and while there are lots of people lined up to work against trafficking, there are just too many others that are lined up to hurt us.

When we look across the State of Texas, our Attorney General has identified 800 victims in the last 5 years. Half of those were children. Houston is the No. 1 source for calls to the Human Trafficking Hotline. We had the big Mondragon human trafficking ring where 120 women and children were rescued a number of years ago. In Dallas, a 12-year-old was found dancing at the all-nude Dallas Diamonds Cabaret. In Corpus Christi, a 14-year-old found dancing at the Club Cheetah. In Houston, at the Taboo Modeling Studio North, a human trafficking den, we found four 16-year-olds.

We have visited some of these spots, unfortunately, and what we find is that we go into these places and we see women paraded in front of us, women lined along the walls, all with blank faces, all not knowing why they are there. This is something that all of us need to work very, very hard to end because it is heartbreaking, and it is eminently solvable but we are not doing enough to solve it.

Thank you very much.

[The prepared statement of Mr. Sanborn follows:]

PREPARED STATEMENT OF ROBERT SANBORN

MARCH 20, 2014

INTRODUCTION

Texas is both a hub for human trafficking and a leader in the fight against it. The Department of Justice estimates that 1 in 4 human trafficking victims will pass through Texas at some point during their ordeal. Indeed, some of the very factors that make Texas such an extraordinary State also make it a hotbed of human trafficking: A diverse population, numerous airports, interstate highways and international ports, prominent professional sports teams, a popular host site to many National conferences and conventions, and a bustling economy. These attributes, while points of pride, also bring demand for human trafficking to our State and allow traffickers to more easily hide and transport their victims and elude law enforcement.

The federal Trafficking Victims Protection Act of 2000 (TVPA) defines human trafficking as the "recruitment, harboring, transportation, providing or obtaining of a person by means of force, fraud, or coercion for the purpose of a commercial sex act or labor services."[1] Force often takes the form of physical abduction, rapes, beatings, and torture, including the withholding of food, clothing, and other basic necessities. Fraud manifests through offers of a better life, the opportunity to work to make money to support their families, or the chance to obtain an education, which then prove false as victims are trapped and forced to work without pay. In the case of sex trafficking, it also often takes the form of psychological manipulation and the appearance of a romantic relationship. Victims, many of whom were abused prior in their homes before being trafficked, are led to believe that they are worthless and that no one else besides their trafficker will love them, and that they have no choice but to submit to sexual exploitation. Coercion can involve exploitation of an immigrant's unfamiliarity with the language and laws of the United States, verbal and psychological abuse, threats of harm to the victim or the victim's family and friends, threats of deportation, isolation, confiscation of travel and identification documents, and the imposition of debt through inflated fees to the sexually-oriented business or trafficking network.[2] Force, fraud, and coercion are used together to keep a victim subjugated. However, according to the TVPA, force, fraud, or coercion need not be proven to convict a person of trafficking when the victim is a child.[3]

Human trafficking involves two kinds of victims: Domestic or international; and comes in two general forms: Labor or sex trafficking. Domestic victims are most commonly subject to sex trafficking, while labor trafficking is more prominent among international victims. However, there is overlap between these categories, with international victims also being subject to sex trafficking, and domestic victims sometimes involved in labor trafficking. Additionally, labor trafficking can become sex trafficking and vice versa. For instance, a young woman may be forced to work as a waitress or dancer at a strip club or cantina, and then be transitioned into sexual exploitation as well.

In Texas, the Office of the Attorney General reports that between 2007 and 2012, it identified almost 700 human trafficking-related incidences, involving almost 800 victims. About half the victims were not U.S. citizens, while the other half were Americans being trafficked domestically. Almost half of the victims were children.

Vishalie's story epitomizes the experience of many international victims of human trafficking. Vishalie was a young woman from India who came to the United States to work as a nanny to support her widowed mother and four younger siblings. She answered a newspaper advertisement in India offering a chance to work in the United States and make enough money to send home. She was offered a job but the terms changed without notice as soon as she arrived in the United States. Her passport was confiscated, and she was sent to work for another family in New Jersey. She was forced to work long hours as a nanny and domestic servant, but did not receive any pay and was not permitted to leave the home alone.

---

[1] 22 U.S.C. § 7101 et seq. (2002).
[2] Id.
[3] Id.

A typical situation for a domestic victim might sound like Sarah's story. Sarah was a 17-year-old girl who ran away from home in rural Ohio because her mother and stepfather were alcoholics and she was neglected at home.[4] She was approached by a 30-year-old man while walking to the store alone who asked her why she looked so upset, and offered to take her to get her nails done to cheer her up.[5] She agreed, and over the next couple of months, he took her out to eat, gave her compliments, and acted like a caring boyfriend.[6] He asked her to move in with him, but after a month of living together he said he could not afford the rent and asked her to engage in commercial sex with older men to pay the bills.[7] Sarah was uncomfortable, but was adamantly against returning home and wanted to please him, so she allowed him to begin prostituting her.[8]

A number of prominent busts involving human trafficking illustrate the problem in Texas. The Maria Bonita Cantina in Houston, Texas, which was owned and operated by Gerardo Salazar Tecuapacho, was busted in 2005. Salazar earned the nickname "El Gallo" by branding his female victims with his trademark rooster. Salazar lured young women from Mexico to leave their homes to travel to Houston under false pretenses of love, marriage, and legitimate job opportunities. Upon arrival in Houston, the women were forced into a life of sexual slavery in the cantina. In 2005, one of Salazar's teenage victims called a domestic violence hotline and told rescuers that she had been brutally beaten and sold in the cantina. Upon indictment, Salazar fled to Mexico where he was eventually arrested and remains while the United States seeks extradition.

Also in 2005, Maximino Mondragon was convicted in the bust of one of the Nation's largest sex trafficking rings. For over a decade, Mondragon ran a ring of cantinas in northwest Houston where he held women and girls lured to this country with the promise of legitimate employment, but quickly forced into prostitution upon their arrival. The women and girls were held captive by constant surveillance and threats of violence to themselves and their families back in Latin America if they attempted to escape. Mondragon controlled the women and girls' money, their clothes, their movements, and even subjected the women to forced abortions. A total of 120 women were rescued from Mondragon's cantinas by law enforcement. Mondragon was sentenced to 13 years in prison and ordered to pay $1.7 million in restitution to his victims.[9]

In 2007, Diamonds Cabaret, an all-nude strip club in Dallas, Texas, was allowed to stay open even after police found they had hired a 12-year-old girl as a stripper.[10] The girl had run away from home and was picked up by a trafficker and a Diamonds Cabaret dancer. They offered her a place to stay, but told her she had to earn her keep, and drove her to the strip club. The club hired her even though she was unable to show valid identification. The girl eventually ran away from her trafficker as he slept, and he ultimately faced Federal charges for felony sexual performance of a child. However, Diamonds Cabaret remained open due to a loophole in the Dallas ordinances, which had no provision allowing officials to shut it down for employing a minor.[11]

In another domestic case involving a minor victim, Club Cheetah in Corpus Christi, Texas, which hired a 14-year-old trafficking victim as a nude dancer, sued the girl and her family after she was rescued from her trafficker.[12] The girl was kidnapped from a San Antonio homeless shelter, sexually assaulted, and then sold for sex at Club Cheetah.[13] Her trafficker pleaded guilty to four counts of aggravated sexual assault in 2010, but Club Cheetah, rather than face criminal penalties, sued the girl and her family in civil court.[14] The club claimed the girl caused damages including loss of revenue, a Texas Alcoholic Beverage Commission investigation, and

[4] *Survivor Stories—Sarah*, POLARIS PROJECT, *http://www.polarisproject.org/what-we-do/client-services/survivor-stories/465-sarah-domestic-minor-sex-trafficking* (last visited Dec. 11, 2012).
[5] Id.
[6] Id.
[7] Id.
[8] Id.
[9] Lise Olsen, *Houston Sex-Trafficking Ringleader Gets 13 Years in Prison*, Hous. Chron. (Apr. 27, 2009), *http://www.chron.com/news/article/Houston-sex-trafficking-ringleader-gets-13-years-1735028.php* (last visited Nov. 1, 2012).
[10] *Lost Girl*, Newsweek, Apr. 3, 2008, *http://www.thedailybeast.com/newsweek/2008/04/03/lost-girl.html* (last visited Nov. 1, 2012).
[11] Id.
[12] Janine Reyes, *Adult Club Sues Alleged Victim, Teen and Family Countersue in Court*, KRISTV.COM, Feb. 29, 2012, *http://www.kristv.com/news/adult-club-sues-alleged-victim-teen-and-family-countersue-in-court/* (last visited Nov. 1, 2012).
[13] Id.
[14] Id.

65

loss of standing and reputation in the community, and asked for $25,000 in damages, court costs, and attorney's fees.[15] The girl's family countersued the club for negligence, seeking damages for her bodily injury and sickness including lost peace of mind, depression, neurosis, nervousness, weight loss, nightmares, irritability, upset stomach, sleep loss, and anxiety.[16] Club Cheetah eventually withdrew their suit in response to the girl's family's countersuit.[17]

In a particularly large trafficking bust in Houston, Texas in 2009, an investigation by the Innocence Lost Task Force of the FBI and the Houston Police Department as part of the Innocence Lost National Initiative resulted in the arrest and charging of five men and one woman with a number of crimes, including conspiracy to traffic women and children for the purposes of commercial sex; sex trafficking of children; and sex trafficking by force, fraud, and coercion.[18] The victims were brought to Houston from other States, including Florida, Kansas, Arizona, and Nevada in one of three business fronts owned and operated by the gang, which included a business operating under the name "Taboo Modeling Studio North." Four 16-year-old minors were among the victims rescued from these operations, including one teenager abducted while walking down the street in Kansas. All of the victims were American citizens, and were beaten routinely and not permitted to keep the profits from their exploitation.

In all situations of human trafficking, whether international or domestic, most victims do not know where to turn to for help. Even when law enforcement gets involved and they are removed from their traffickers, services for victims are severely lacking, and too-often victims are treated as criminals themselves.

SEXUALLY-ORIENTED BUSINESSES

As the second-largest and fastest-growing criminal industry in the world, the singular purpose of trafficking in persons is to generate illicit profits for the traffickers.[19] How do traffickers translate their control of the trafficking victim into profits? There are many different methods, but one of the most prevalent is through sexually-oriented businesses. These businesses dovetail perfectly with the trafficker's intent to profit from the exploitation of victims, as they provide a ready-made market. While some sexually-oriented businesses, such as strip clubs, are easily identifiable as sexually-oriented, others are established as "massage parlors," "modeling studios," or other non-sexual business entities in an effort to disguise their true identities as brothels and venues for labor and sex trafficking.

Traffickers sometimes directly own a sexually-oriented business, or simply make financial arrangements with the owners and managers as a way to facilitate the marketing and exploitation of their victims. Essentially, businesses provide the venue for the traffickers to market and sell their products, and traffickers then pay a portion of their profits to the business owners and operators. Also complicit in these illegal business ventures are the clients, or "johns," who patronize the establishments for the purpose of commercial sex. Like any commercial enterprise, human trafficking is fueled by the law of supply and demand—but for the customers willing to pay for commercial sex, these illegal businesses would not be in existence.

It is important to note that not all sexually-oriented businesses are illicit fronts for commercial sex and human trafficking. State and local laws expressly authorize the establishment of sexually-oriented businesses, and legitimate sexually-oriented businesses that are properly licensed and operating within the parameters of regulation exist throughout the country. The problems associated with human trafficking arise when sexually-oriented businesses operate beyond the scope of legal boundaries, serving as venues for prostitution and other illegal activities. The prevalence of these illegal sexually-oriented businesses varies from State to State, and even between localities within States. For instance, in Texas' Greater Houston area, while there are over 300 sexually-oriented businesses, fewer than 20 are licensed as such. Not all of these 300-plus businesses are involved in the illegal commercial sex trade; some may not meet the requirements of the county or city ordinance and therefore

---

[15] Id.
[16] Id.
[17] Id.
[18] U.S. Attorney's Office S. Dist. of Tex., *Remaining Defendants Convicted in District's Largest Sex Trafficking Case* (Oct. 4, 2012) available at *http://www.fbi.gov/houston/press-releases/2012/remaining-defendants-convicted-in-districts-largest-domestic-sex-trafficking-case* (last visited Nov. 1, 2012).
[19] Houston Rescue & Restore Coalition, *What is Human Trafficking?*, *http://www.houstonrr.org/human-trafficking/what-is-human-trafficking/* (last visited Nov. 1, 2012).

do not seek licensure, while others are indeed illicit fronts for commercial sex.[20] Several of these unlicensed businesses have been identified and shut down after multiple instances of prostitution, sexual assault, and human trafficking have occurred. However, many continue to operate unchecked. Treasures, one of the most well-known and notorious strip clubs in Houston, is not licensed as a sexually-oriented business, and has been cited dozens of times for prostitution, drug use, and public lewdness. Despite efforts by the city to shut it down as a public nuisance, the club has avoided closure.

Sexually-oriented businesses come in a wide variety of models and are continually mutating to avoid regulations and detection from law enforcement. Some of the most common forms of sexually-oriented businesses include: Cantinas, strip clubs, massage parlors, modeling studios, tea houses, and hostess lounges. Often, sexually-oriented businesses operate within racial or ethnic networks that share similar characteristics in terms of their operating structure and the trafficker and victim profiles. For instance, Asian sexually-oriented businesses such as massage parlors, hostess clubs, and tea rooms may be connected by a criminal organization that runs a variety of sexually-oriented businesses and rotates women between facilities. Latino sexually-oriented businesses take the form of residential brothels, escort services, and cantinas. Both Asian and Latino sex trafficking networks primarily exploit immigrant women and girls, capitalizing on their undocumented status, unfamiliarity with the country, and economic desperation. Notwithstanding the prevalence of racially exclusive trafficking networks, often domestic and international networks comingle. Strip clubs, for example, may provide an avenue for organized crime enterprises to funnel trafficking victims from Eastern Europe, while also serving as a venue for domestic trafficking.

The internet provides an easy means for traffickers to directly prostitute their victims and to advertise their sexually-oriented businesses. Human trafficking also thrives on relatively unregulated internet sites such as Backpage.com, Eros.com, Rubmaps.com, and Craiglist.com, and the internet is the No. 1 platform where traffickers, pimps, and johns buy and sell women and girls for sex.[21] Ads may appear to be posted by an individual who is operating independently but are often created by, or at the direction of, a trafficker.[22] Sexually-oriented businesses, particularly massage parlors, heavily advertise on the internet. On any given day in Houston, just one internet site could feature over 300 ads for sex and almost 200 ads for sexually-oriented businesses. While impossible to confirm exact numbers, it is safe to say that a large proportion of these ads feature victims of human trafficking, and at least 3 dozen ads per day feature girls who appear to be under 18.

THE FIGHT AGAINST HUMAN TRAFFICKING

While Texas does face significant challenges regarding the prevalence of human trafficking within our borders, we are also in many ways leaders in the fight against human trafficking. The Texas Legislature has been resolute and effective in passing laws to combat trafficking, and since 2007, has enacted 28 anti-trafficking bills. Many of these laws strengthen the penalties for traffickers and johns in order to deter and punish those who would exploit victims. Recently, the State legislature has also focused on providing services for victims, to ensure that they have the resources available to them to recover and rebuild their lives.

The training of law enforcement is crucial and has been very successful as a result of a 2009 bill that mandated training in human trafficking for all newly-licensed police officers and all officers wishing to advance in rank. The training ensures that law enforcement is better able to detect human trafficking and more adequately prepared to deal with victims. A bill passed just last year in the 83rd Session builds on this success by requiring that the Texas Education Agency, the Department of Family and Protective Services, and the Health and Human Services Commission create curriculum to train doctors, nurses, emergency medical services personnel, teachers, school counselors and administrators, and child welfare workers to identify and assist victims of human trafficking. It is critically important that these professionals receive education around human trafficking because they are often the first points of contact for victims to receive help. Without the proper training, we run the risk that these victims will fall through the cracks and not be identified and rescued.

---

[20] CHILDREN AT RISK, Study on Sexually Oriented Businesses in the Greater Houston Area, August 2012, *http://childrenatrisk.org/wp-content/uploads/2010/11/State-of-Human-Trafficking-in-Texas-FINAL.pdf* (last visited Dec. 17, 2012).

[21] Polaris Project, *Human Trafficking-Internet Based, http://www.polarisproject.org/human-trafficking/sex-trafficking-in-the-us/internet-based* (last visited Nov. 1, 2012).

[22] Id.

As Texas focuses more on the needs of victims of human trafficking, it is apparent that not enough residential shelters exist to provide comprehensive services to these victims, not only in Texas but across the country. Funding is desperately needed to assist in the establishment of such shelters, which can be quite costly considering the wide range of medical, emotional, educational, and economic needs victims present. However, as more and more individuals and organizations become aware of the victims' needs and seek to start shelters, it is imperative that standards are in place for facilities that provide services to victims. Texas addressed this need in 2013 by passing a bill that mandates minimum standards to ensure that such shelters address the special needs of trafficking victims and provide adequate services. Such standards are needed across the country.

Texas, like a number of other States including Washington and New Jersey, have attempted to regulate internet sites that provide a venue for human traffickers to exploit their victims, but have been severely limited in their ability to hold internet service providers liable by the Federal Communications Decency Act ("CDA"). While the purpose of the CDA is to preserve the dynamic nature of the internet and to protect internet service providers from liability for the content posted on their sites by users, it is proving to constitute a significant barrier to States seeking to regulate websites that profit from and promote human trafficking. We need Congressional action to amend the CDA to eliminate the loophole that allows trafficking to flourish on the internet, immune from State regulation by Federal law.

CONCLUSION

Sadly, many of the reasons that Texas is a great place to live also make it vulnerable to the proliferation of human trafficking. International and domestic trafficking are both widespread in Texas, aided by the presence of many unregulated sexually-oriented businesses and the ease the internet provides for traffickers to exploit their victims. However, the Texas Legislature has been aggressive and diligent in passing legislation aimed at eliminating trafficking from the State. More still needs to be done on a National level to address funding and standards for safe houses for victims, and to curb the use of the internet as a marketplace for trafficking. Yet we are confident as awareness grows of this horrible and widespread crime, our National leaders will be in the forefront of the fight against it.

Chairman McCAUL. Thank you, Doctor. Thank you for your passion on this issue.

Dr. Isaac, you are recognized for 5 minutes.

STATEMENT OF REENA ISAAC, M.D., ASSISTANT PROFESSOR OF PEDIATRICS, BAYLOR COLLEGE OF MEDICINE AND ATTENDING PHYSICIAN, CHILD ABUSE PEDIATRICS SECTION OF THE EMERGENCY DEPARTMENT, TEXAS CHILDREN'S HOSPITAL

Dr. ISAAC. Thank you, Chairman McCaul, Ranking Member Sheila Jackson Lee, and committee Members.

Health care providers are one of the few groups of professionals likely to interface with victims of human trafficking while they are still in the control of the criminals who profit from them. A study in 2005 found that 28 percent of the victims came into contact with the health care system at least one time during their captivity. This represents a critical opportunity for identification and intervention. Health care providers are in a unique position to screen for victims of trafficking and provide important medical and psychological care for victims, as well as introduce critical services and supports that may enable them rescue and reintegration back into society.

It is estimated that 100,000 children are in the sex trade in the United States each year. Children at highest risk for victimization are the homeless youth, throwaway, and runaway children, children with low self-esteem, children who are neglected and abused, or any child that seeks love. Recognizing these children as high-risk may serve as an important prevention strategy and an area where health care professionals may also be in a position to intervene and redirect.

One of the challenges of the health care worker is identifying this vulnerable and silent population. Some of the recognized barriers to detecting victims include isolation from others, victim reluctance to disclose the abuse, continual surveillance by traffickers, lack of awareness of even being a victim, and basic distrust of adults and mistrust of authorities. Given this understanding, victims do not readily self-identify themselves as victims and training on recognizing the signs is crucial, and development of skills to facilitate identification is necessary.

Given the scope and breadth of the problems faced by this marginalized population, it has become clear that the issue of human trafficking is not only a human rights issue but also a global health issue. Some of the issues that we see with these survivors are issues related to mental health, physical trauma, reproductive issues, substance abuse, and infectious diseases.

Some of the mental health problems in children may including low self-esteem, suicidal thoughts, and poor academic achievement. Drug addiction and substance abuse may also manifest during their years of captivity. In one study involving trafficked women, it was revealed that 69 percent suffered from post-traumatic stress disorder.

Physical trauma can result from forced manual labor or from the direct physical violence by the trafficker or clients in an effort to control and dominate the victim.

Victims of the sex trafficking industry are at high risk for acquiring multiple sexually transmitted diseases, including HIV infection. Pregnancy, complications from unsafe termination procedures, and complicated infections of the genital tract may also present.

Seeking to respond to the call for additional training of health care professionals, a local grassroots, nonprofit organization, The Houston Rescue and Restore Coalition, adopted a curriculum-planning project named Health Professionals and Human Trafficking: Look Beneath the Surface, H.E.A.R. Your Patient. This program known locally as the H.E.A.R. Project provides not only the knowledge and awareness of human trafficking to health care professionals, but also builds the skills for identification and referral of potential victims of human trafficking. This project, which began in 2010, has been instrumental in successfully training hundreds of medical professionals in the Houston area and is in the process of evolving into a multimedia training program with the expectation for a much larger reach Nationally.

In addition to the identification of victims, health care professionals can be instrumental in the criminal investigation and prosecution of traffickers and clients in the collection of the patient's historical information required for diagnosis and treatment and forensic evidence. Medical professionals with particular expertise in child abuse and child sexual abuse may serve as expert witnesses in the courtroom. In these capacities, the profession can provide a voice to the voiceless.

The victims of these crimes have experienced incredible physical, emotional, and psychological traumas. Instead of a childhood filled

69

with laughter and promise, child victims, many of whom have been forced across borders from their familiar homelands into our Nation, have been subjected to and experienced unimaginable horrors that strip them of their own identities and the very beauty of what it means to be human.

I would propose to the committee to consider the allowance of funding to enhance collaborative training of health care professionals in our efforts to identify and intervene on behalf of these victims.

I thank the committee for this opportunity to speak on behalf of the medical professionals involved in the care of these children.

[The prepared statement of Dr. Isaac follows:]

PREPARED STATEMENT OF REENA ISAAC

MARCH 20, 2014

Health care providers are one of the few groups of professionals likely to interface with victims of human trafficking while they are still under the control of the criminals who profit from them. A study in 2005 found that 28% of victims came into contact with the health care system at least one time during their captivity. This represents a critical opportunity for identification and intervention. Health care providers are in a unique position to screen for victims of trafficking and provide important medical and psychological care for victims, as well, as introduce critical services and supports that may enable them rescue and re-integration back into society. Front-line medical care centers such as emergency departments, primary care pediatric centers, family practice offices, reproductive health clinics, public health clinics, are most likely to interface with victims seeking acute and basic medical care. Efforts to optimize these opportunities for intervention require additional training for identification of victims by medical and nursing personnel, as well as, instruction on available community resources for support, services, and protection of the victim.

Human trafficking encompasses many different aspects: International vs. domestic victims, adult vs. child victims, and labor vs. sex trafficking victims. It is estimated that 100,000 children are in the sex trade in the United States each year. Children at highest risk for victimization are the homeless youth, throwaway and runaway children, children with low self-esteem, children who are neglected and abused, or any child that seeks love. Recognizing these children as high risk may serve as an important prevention strategy and an area where health care professionals may also be in a position to intervene and redirect.

One of the challenges for the health care worker is identifying this vulnerable, silent population. Some of the recognized barriers to detecting victims include: (1) Isolation from others, (2) victim reluctance to disclose abuse, (3) continual surveillance by traffickers, (4) lack of awareness of being a victim, and (5) basic distrust of adults and mistrust of authorities. Given this understanding, victims do not readily self-identify themselves as victims and training on recognizing the signs is crucial and development of skills to facilitate identification is necessary.

The trafficking victim-patient carries a unique set of health care needs that, once identified, can be properly assessed and addressed. Given the scope and breadth of the problems faced by this marginalized population, it has become clear that the issue of human trafficking is not only a human rights issue but also a global public health issue. The role of the health care professional is an important one on many levels.

The possible signs and symptoms in a trafficked victim's presentation that may alert health professionals are vast:

Mental health.—Children with exposure to trauma typically experience affective, behavioral, and cognitive problems. Increased incidences of acute anxiety and stress disorder, affective disorders, conduct disorders, and personality disorders have also been recognized. Other mental health problems may include low self-esteem, suicidal ideation, poor academic achievement, and poor interpersonal relationship quality. Drug addiction and substance abuse may also manifest during their years in captivity. Research of 130 trafficked women revealed that 69% suffered from posttraumatic stress disorder. Sex trafficking and sexual exploitation appear to carry a greater increased risk for adverse health outcomes than with a homelessness or runaway status alone.

Physical trauma.—Physical trauma can result from forced manual labor or from direct physical violence by the trafficker or clients in an effort to control and dominate the victim. Any form of bodily injury may be a result of extreme physical stress. Traffickers may beat, kick, choke, burn, or cut victims, as a way to control and manipulate them. Cigarette burns, fractures, bruises, and burns are common injuries of physical violence. Tattoos found on the body may serve to identify the victim as property of a particular trafficker, in effect branding the victim as a mere product of commerce.

Reproductive and genitourinary issues.—Children, adolescents, and adults who are victims of the sex trafficking industry are at high risk for acquiring multiple sexually transmitted diseases, including HIV infection. Sexually exploited adolescents are at greater risk of HIV infection than adults due, in part, to the greater levels of violence toward minor victims and the anatomic variances between the two. Pregnancy, complications from unsafe termination procedures, and complicated infections of the genital tract may also present.

Substance abuse.—Traffickers may introduce drug use for their victims to keep them compliant or passive during their time of captivity. Children with pre-existing addictions may be recruited into exploitation in their attempt to obtain drugs. Other victims may use drugs and alcohol to help them cope with the stress of their lives.

Infectious diseases.—In addition to being at risk for acquiring sexually transmitted infections, human trafficking victims may be forced to live and work under unsanitary conditions, placing them at risk for various infections including tuberculosis.

Seeking to respond to the call by both National and Houston-based community needs assessments for additional training of health care professionals in the identification and intervention of human trafficking victims, a local grassroots non-profit organization, The Houston Rescue and Restore Coalition (HRRC) adopted a curriculum-planning project that was constructed and organized by a graduate student researcher from the UT School of Public Health and guided in the medical approach and practical delivery by a Texas Children's Hospital physician advisor and other professionals. This program, *Health Professionals and Human Trafficking: Look Beneath the Surface, H.E.A.R. Your Patient,* provides not only the knowledge and awareness of human trafficking to health professionals, but also builds the skills of identification and referral of a potential victim of human trafficking.

The components of the program include: Section 1: Fundamental information on human trafficking (definition, types, prevalence, myths, challenges, importance of health professionals). Section 2: The building of the skill set required to approach and critically assess details of a case that may involve a potential victim of human trafficking is fostered. A case study introduces the challenges and potential indicators for a suspected victim. The introduction of the H.E.A.R. acronym is incorporated. The acronym outlines the steps of how to properly identify a victim and refer and report.

H: Human Trafficking and Health Professionals

E: Examine History, Examine Body, Examine Emotion

A: Ask specific questions:

"Is anyone forcing you to do anything you do not want to do?"

"Can you leave your job or situation if you want?"

"Have you or your family been threatened if you try to leave?"

R: Review options, Refer, Report.

Section 3: Three case studies with different scenarios with various barriers in which the learners must appropriately identify, refer, and report their patients. Currently the project has evolved into having these case studies as video vignettes to further visually depict the challenges of these cases in a health care setting. Information regarding the available supports and services for the identified survivor's basic needs and safety are provided. In the cases involving children, human trafficking is a form of child abuse for those victims under the age of 18 and any suspicion of its activity involves the mandated reporting to law enforcement and child protection agencies.

This project which began in 2010 has been instrumental in successfully training hundreds of medical and nursing professionals in the Houston area and is in the process of evolving into a multi-media training program with the expectation for a much larger reach Nationally. The global community has become aware of the numerous challenges faced by human trafficking victims. Once contact is made between the victim and health care professionals, the opportunity then exists to identify, treat, and assist the victims. Once their medical and psychological needs are assessed and treatment offered, many of the other recognized immediate needs of these persons including the basics of housing, food, medical needs, safety, and legal services can addressed.

In addition to the identification of victims, health care professionals can be instrumental in the criminal investigation and prosecution of traffickers and clients in the collection of patient historical information (required for diagnosis and treatment) and forensic evidence. Meticulous documentation of findings and, in some cases, photo-documentation of injuries may assist in bolstering a case for criminal investigation and prosecution. Medical professionals may be asked to provide medical knowledge of the science, medical record review, or provide information of their personal evaluation of the child. Medical professionals with particular expertise in child abuse and child sexual abuse may serve as expert witnesses in the court room. In these capacities, the profession can provide a voice to the voiceless.

The medical and nursing communities are important stakeholders in the role of identifying and victims of this hidden population. The front-line physicians and nurses, and specialized forensic physicians and nurses, and sexual assault nurse examiners are solid and available community resources throughout the country and may play a vital role in the prevention, protection, and prosecution of these cases by collaborating and communicating with the other dedicated professionals in a multidisciplinary manner and bringing these children back into the light.

The victims of these crimes have experienced incredible physical, emotional, and psychological traumas. Instead of a childhood filled with laughter and promise, child victims, many of whom having been forced to cross borders from their familiar homelands into our Nation, have been subjected to and experienced unimaginable horrors that strip them of their own identities and the very beauty of what it means to be human. I would propose for the committee to consider the allowance of funding to enhance collaborative training of health care professionals in our efforts to identify and intervene on behalf of these victims. A small allocation of the monetary proceeds of seized assets of disrupted trafficking rings can perhaps be one area where such funding could assist in the continued development and delivery of needed training programs as I have described. I thank the committee for this opportunity to speak on behalf of the medical professionals involved in the care of these children.

Chairman MCCAUL. Thank you, Dr. Isaac.

The Chairman now recognizes Ms. Briggs.

STATEMENT OF CHERYL BRIGGS, FOUNDER AND CHIEF EXECUTIVE OFFICER, MISSION AT SERENITY RANCH

Ms. BRIGGS. I would like to thank the Chairman and the committee for the honor to speak here today, along with the distinguished panelists.

In 2009, I was going to Sam Houston State University and I was trying to obtain my undergraduate degree. I had a sociology class. In that class, our assignment for that semester was to do a paper on a sociology issue in current news. So I was in the library researching, and about a couple hours into it, I found these words "human trafficking." Probably like everybody else in this room before they were educated more, I thought those poor people from other countries, those children in Thailand and Bangkok and Asia. That is what I thought of.

When I began to read more, I thought—I was drawn to it. Then I thought, wait a minute. This ain't new. This happened to me when I was a teenager in the 1970's. So it may have looked a little bit different because we did not have the internet. We did not have craigslist, backpage. We did not have any of that kind of stuff in the 1970's in the dinosaur age.

So as a survivor, I believe that we offer a unique insight into the victimization and rehabilitation process that these children and these victims deserve. I feel like, in working with different agencies, that collaboration is absolutely vital.

I must say this, Congressman Poe. The first time I heard you speak was at the Crime Stoppers conference a couple years ago. At that time, you mentioned human trafficking, and at that time, you mentioned especially about the international victims. So I see that you have been under an education process that includes our own citizens.

So the Justice for Victims of Trafficking Act—I really think that there are some important points in that that I agree with strongly, and that is, that No. 1, it creates a fund for domestic victims to allow them the opportunity to get treatment on the same level as every other victim, international or domestic. There are no victims who are more important than the other, who are more hurt than the other. They are all victims. So also allowing them to be certified as a victim of severe human trafficking actually speeds up the process for them to get the services that they need in a timely manner.

I also believe that—and the other thing was the importance of—it was all addressed on the demand side, but it is the importance of knowing that you increase the definition of trafficker by adding the word "solicitation," which then also opens the door for—I call them rapists that are purchasing sex from these children and these people. It allows them to be included in that Federal statute.

So in working with domestic minor trafficking victims, it is very imperative that we protect the most vulnerable in our society and that would be our children and our mentally ill and our handicapped. As far as the children go, there are many, many people in our country who really, really with all their heart want to help these people. The problem is that because they have no survivor involved in their organization or on a consultation basis that helps understand certain things that you cannot understand unless you have been a victim and how to transition from that victim to survivor.

It took me 30 long years to get that done, and it was piecing together services throughout my life for domestic violence, drug addiction, and many, many things. When I was trafficked at 13½, I was given an IV drug addiction to MDA which is a component, main component, of the drug Ecstasy today. It is a hallucinogenic and opiate combination, and the reason that I was drugged was so I would be very pliable and good for child pornography. So I am also glad that we are adding child pornography to those definitions.

I would like to say that I want to address the supply and demand. So human trafficking is like any other economic system. It is supply-and-demand. We have mentioned this several times today. But what I wanted to point out was Dr. Melissa Farley with Prostitution Research Center in San Francisco did a study in Sweden on the prostitution problem there. Now, in Sweden, prostitution is illegal. But the Swedish government decided that they would take a new approach, and I think it is something that we can learn from. That is, when someone was arrested for prostitution, they were offered services that helped them change their life because like Adrian Garcia said, nobody grows up and goes, you know, I think I am going to be a prostitute because I do not want to pay taxes. I mean, nobody says that. We want to grow up and be princesses. We want to grow up and be doctors and lawyers. But there are so many kids that do not get that opportunity. Children do not run to; they run from. So 80 percent of the children on the streets are there, the same reason I was because of the abuse at home that you can no longer take. It hurts less to be abused by someone you do not love.

I would also like to say that in that Swedish model, they actually cut trafficking in half in 1 year because you cannot sell a 14-year-old girl if there is not someone standing there with the money to buy her. If the johns are afraid, the rapists are afraid of being publicly humiliated—and Judge Poe did this when he was a judge—was that public shame. Hey, I am a thief. I stole from the store. We need to learn from that, because guess what? That is appropriate. We have been using social shame in civilization since the beginning of time.

The deal is, though, once that social shame is over, then they need to be able to get the resources that they also need to heal. Maybe they are addicted to pornography. Maybe they were abused. Hurt people hurt people. So we never know where that line is going to end.

I do not know how much time I have left, but I also wanted to comment on the picture that we sometimes paint. It was mentioned before about the child or the woman or the man and the boy that is chained to a bed and walked through a cold shower once a day, fed a bologna sandwich, and abused by people after people, very broken, malnourished, beaten people. I think we need to be very careful about that picture that we paint because that may happen in a very small percentage of cases.

What you need to look out for is someone like me. What you need to look out for is your granddaughter. What you need to look out for is your neighbor, a girl in Sunday school. That is what you need to look out for, because guess what? There are children in our high schools that are being trafficked by kids in high school. They think they are in love with a man—with a boy, and they have their first sexual experience with him, and guess what? He is videotaping it. Then he says to her: Listen, I got you on tape. Your parents are going to hate you. You are going to be humiliated. I am going to show it to everybody unless you do this.

Now, there was a friend of mine. Her name is Teresa Flores out of Ohio, and she wrote a book called "The Slave Next Door." How, she was trafficked. She was in an upper middle class family in Ohio I believe or Detroit, one of the two. But that happened to her. It was a good home. There was no abuse going on at all. There was nothing to indicate to anybody. But she went to school by day. She was an honor roll student. When the lights went out at night, they were outside her window and she went out the window and she did what she had to do all night long because she was afraid of the shame and rejection. So we end up allowing these victims to carry the shame that does not belong to them.

The last thing I think that I really want to address is that there are many things that we can improve on in the State of Texas and in our Nation. But what I would like to see is that I would like to see more restored survivor involvement in the process because, like I said, it is kind of like an alcoholic. You really cannot understand another—alcoholic understands another alcoholic. It is the same system no matter how you go, what social group you are looking at. It is about the process of identification. It is about sharing a common pain. It is about our humanity. We cannot continue to let this happen. So why are 100,000 kids a year on the street? Where are those emergency shelters for those kids so they have a safe place to go, maybe a protected center? Because, guess what? They get put in CPS, and 80 percent of those kids are at higher risk of being victimized.

I was in CPS. I was in foster care. I was in a detention center. I was in the Youth Commission. They never ever could fix the problem. They just shipped me to somebody else to do it because they did not understand it.

So if there is anything that I or Kathryn or other survivors that are working in this field can do to help you do what you need to be able to do that I do not have the authority to do, please let me know because I am making myself available.

I want to thank you so much.

[The prepared statement of Ms. Briggs follows:]

PREPARED STATEMENT OF CHERYL BRIGGS

MARCH 20, 2014

As a survivor of Domestic Minor Sex Trafficking (DMST), I feel I have a unique insight on the victimization and rehabilitation process that non-survivors may not have. From this standpoint, I know the specialized services a victim needs to transform to survivor.

The proposed Justice for Victims of Trafficking Act, currently in Congress seeks to clarify portions of the Trafficked Victims Protection Act (TVPA) in changing the definition of trafficking to include solicitation by buyers of trafficking victims. It also creates a Domestic Trafficking Victims Fund (DTVF) and allows domestic victims to obtain certification as a victim of severe human trafficking and thereby, providing a victim quicker access to funds and services. This fund will increase Federal resources for domestic trafficking victims up to $30 million per year, among many other important points.

While there have been recommended Best Practices developed for DMST, there are no required minimal standards of care. While the majority of residential treatment programs for minors are licensed by the Health and Human Services Commission, this in no way qualifies the facility for offering trafficking services. I feel that it is of upmost importance that minimal standards be developed and required for any agency receiving Federal or State funding. This population especially minors are very vulnerable to manipulation, exploitation, and are at great risk of re-victimization by agencies that want to help that are not qualified to do so. We have an obligation to protect the most vulnerable in our society and assure that services provided are adequate, sufficient, and timely.

The final point I would like to make is human trafficking, like any other industry, runs on an economics of supply and demand. It has been proven through studies by Dr. Melissa Farley of the Prostitution and Research Center in San Francisco, through a study in Sweden, that providing prostituted women with services and prosecuting "johns", decreased the number of trafficking victims by half. If we focus not only on the criminal enterprises in which trafficking occurs but the purchasers of the victims themselves, we would greatly reduce the supply. If through fear of public shame and/or increased prosecution of statutes, "johns" became afraid, that would create less demand which would automatically reflect in a decrease supply.

Chairman MCCAUL. Well, thank you.

[Applause.]

Chairman MCCAUL. Thank you for that powerful testimony, and we do look forward to working with you.

The Chairman now recognizes Ms. Griffin-Townsend.

STATEMENT OF KATHRYN GRIFFIN-TOWNSEND, FOUNDER, WE'VE BEEN THERE DONE THAT REENTRY PROGRAM, HARRIS COUNTY SHERIFF'S OFFICE

Ms. GRIFFIN-TOWNSEND. Chairman McCaul, Ranking Member Jackson Lee, and all of the Members of the committee, thank you for holding this very important hearing today here in Houston, Texas, which is the epicenter of America as we look at human trafficking.

Congresswoman Lee, your leadership today reaffirms American values of freedom and equality by addressing this issue in the United States Congress, which strengthens hope for victims of human trafficking who continue to fight for justice. Thank you. I thank all of you.

I want to also welcome and thank Chairman McCaul for allowing me to begin to tell you about this story. I am a survivor of domestic human trafficking, and now I am free to live life.

I have had the distinct honor for more than a decade to work with a certain slice of our population. I am referring to those men, women, and children who have fallen prey to international and domestic human trafficking, prostitution, and sexual slavery. This truly has been a difficult endeavor. However, thankfully through evidence-based rehabilitation, this difficult task has resulted in tremendous success for those whom we have helped.

Allow me to describe briefly the process. The rehabilitation of those who have been sold for sex is a very long trauma-based process, and it can take up to 4 years. Nearly always, survivors and victims of human trafficking and sex slavery suffer from some form of abuse. While substance abuse, sexual abuse, mental abuse, and/ or physical abuse are most prevalent, many other psychological dysfunctions and cognitive issues may also be present. Through my experiences, I have found that all of these issues are best resolved by treating them with a specific protocol.

First, their trust must be gained while allowing the victim time to understand that they are not alone in their plight and that someone else that has been there and done that and others are truly invested in their best interest and not patronizing the victim to take advantage of them again. Only then can true change begin by moving the victim even closer to becoming the valuable productive citizen in society they at this stage simply just do not know how to be. Many in this population have never had the opportunity to know that they count in this life. Codependency, abandonment issues, and the "poor old me" syndrome plagues this population. Fears such as homelessness and the stigmas that attach themselves to this population are devastating. Guilt and shame attach to the lives of these individuals as easily as gum attaches itself to the bottom of your shoe.

For this group, rehabilitation is a must. We at the Harris County Sheriff's Office, under the leadership of Sheriff Adrian Garcia, have opened up a new world of hope and success for the thousands who come through the We've Been There Done That program.

As participants in the reentry program, these victims are protected by being kept away from their drug dealers, pimps, sugar daddies, johns, and predators long enough to begin the deprogramming of the damage they have suffered. This is a population that is accustomed to constantly being on the run, chased from one predator to another, as a lion would chase a deer until they fall again and again in a perpetual loop of tragedy. It is easier to deprogram these clients while they are in a facility, not necessarily a jail facility, but a secure facility where they do not have access to drugs, pimps, sugar daddies, johns, and predators where finally they have a chance to catch their breath and begin to heal.

As a recovery coach, I am able to offer continuous coaching to these individuals for up to 5 years or as long as they need or the individual would want me to coach them. The need for case managers is essential. As desperately needed are housing facilities that can nourish these clients for up to 2 years until they are strong enough and have developed adequate skills to live on their own while still remaining in a rehabilitation program.

The We've Been There Done That program offers this population a program of a minimum of 90 days to 180 days, and it is in the county jail where they receive the intensive deprogramming that is needed to separate them from the environment that they have been trapped within. After this, they are placed in facilities that can help manage their specific needs such as substance abuse, mental abuse, homelessness, et cetera.

Thanks to our student interns from the University of Houston Downtown Criminal Justice Program—they have been a great asset to us volunteering to assist with case management in the Harris County jail. Their work helps us to assure that the clients, when they leave our custody, have exit plans, recovery plans, and their life plans are mapped out for them.

Another component of the program is providing services to those victims who have been caught up in criminal activity because I follow them into the State jail where I continue to work with them, and there I offer a continued support even after they have been released.

You see not all who have begun the process are willing to go into inpatient facilities. Some of them would like to remain employed and support their children or family while they are attending an outpatient treatment option. But based on my experience, the preliminary results indicate treatment drastically increases the success rate, which we have been collecting data here in the last 6 months at the Harris County jail.

It needs to be noted that some of this population will experience bumps in the road. It is to be expected. It is absolutely essential that we fund beds for those who have been identified as victims of international or domestic human trafficking. You see this group is quite familiar with conning, manipulation, lying, stealing, and cheating. But my experience has shown me that the majority of them express guilt about the crimes they committed or were forced to commit and they want to stop this endless loop. They just do not know how. Hurt people hurt people.

What does human trafficking look like? Success stories that have come out. They were children as sex slaves and aged out and ended up and fell into adult prostitution, substance abuse, homelessness, and were stuck on the "poor old me" syndrome. All of these wonderful people are now productive citizens that have returned back into our society.

[Applause.]

Ms. GRIFFIN-TOWNSEND. That is the good alumni from Harris County.

[Laughter.]

Ms. GRIFFIN-TOWNSEND. Not all victims have criminal histories, though.

They come from every race, gender, age, and ethnicity imaginable. The fact is the face of international and domestic human trafficking has multiple faces, and unfortunately, we are introduced to too many different faces on a daily basis. Many victims do not even realize they have been victims of human trafficking. Allow me to reiterate. Hurt people hurt other people.

Thirty-day substance abuse treatment programs are simply not long enough to address social, physical, psychological, and developmental traumas that torment this population. Let me tell you. It takes a lot more than some care packages and some food and clothes. Their need for deprogramming, treatment, and assistance is obligatory. It is mandatory if they are to survive.

Our goal is to stop the recidivism of human trafficking victims from recycling into the criminal justice system and return these rehabilitated victims to the general population as productive members of society with the same inalienable rights that those who have not ever been victimized too often take for granted.

I am committed for the rest of my life to stay on this battlefield, educating, rehabilitating, and teaching the world to appreciate this population while helping as many as I can escape the bondage of human trafficking for the freedom to live free.

I am begging all of you. Please open your hearts and your minds and to help us fight this great fight by helping us to save victims in this silent war. People should not be for sale.

I am available to speak with anyone who would be interested in first-hand information involving this human trafficking epidemic.

Thank you for your time, and I look forward to speaking to you all on this issue.

God bless you and may God bless the United States of America.

[The prepared statement of Ms. Griffin-Townsend follows:]

PREPARED STATEMENT OF KATHRYN GRIFFIN-TOWNSEND

MARCH 20, 2014

First, thank you for the opportunity to address this committee.

I have had the distinct honor for more than a decade to work with a certain slice of our population. I am referring to those men, women, and children who have fallen prey to international and domestic human trafficking, prostitution, and sexual slavery. This truly has been a difficult endeavor, however, thankfully, through evidence-based rehabilitation this difficult task has resulted in tremendous success for those who have been helped.

Allow me to describe briefly the process; the rehabilitation of those who have been sold for sex is a very long trauma-based process, and it can take up to 4 years. Nearly always, survivors and victims of human trafficking and sex slavery suffer from some form of abuse. While substance abuse, sexual abuse, mental abuse, and/ or physical abuse are the most prevalent, many other psychological dysfunctions and cognitive issues may be present themselves as well. Through my experiences, I have found that all of these issues work best by treating them with a specific protocol.

First, their trust must be gained by allowing them time to understand that they are not alone in their plight and that someone else is truly invested in their best interest and not simply patronizing them in order to once again take advantage of them. Only then can true change begin moving them ever closer to becoming the valuable productive citizen in society they at this stage simply don't know how to be. Many in this population have never had an opportunity to know that they count in this life. Codependency, abandonment issues, and "poor-old-me" syndrome becomes major issues for many and plagues this population. Fears such as homelessness and the stigmas that attach themselves to this population are devastating. Guilt and shame attaches itself to the lives of these individuals as easily as gum clings to your shoe.

For this group, rehabilitation is a must. We at the Harris County Sheriff's Office under the leadership of Sheriff Adrian Garcia, have opened up a new world of hope and success for the thousands who have come through the We've Been There Done That program.

I'm sure we agree that it appears that we are punishing victims all over again, but that is simply not the case.

By them present in our reentry program they are instead being protected by being kept away from their drug dealers, pimps, sugar daddies, johns, and predators long enough to begin deprogramming the damage they have suffered. This is a population that is used to constantly being on the run, chased from one predator to another as a lion would chase a deer until they fall again and again in a perpetual loop of tragedy. It is easier to deprogram these clients while they are in a facility where they do not have access to drugs, pimps, sugar daddies, johns, and predators, finally they have the chance to catch a breath and begin to heal.

As their recovery coach, I am able to offer continuous coaching to these individuals for up to 5 years or as long as the individual would like for me to coach them. The need for case managers is essential. Also desperately needed are facilities that can house these clients for up to 2 years until they are strong enough and have developed adequate skills to live on their own, while still remaining in an active rehabilitation program.

The We've Been There Done That program offers this population a program of a minimum of 90 to 180 days in the county jail where they can receive the intensive deprograming that is needed to separate them from the environment they have been trapped within. After this, they are placed in facilities that help manage their specific needs, i.e., substance abuse, mental abuse, homelessness, etc . . .

Student interns from the University of Houston—Downtown Criminal Justice Program have also been a great asset to us volunteering to assist with case management in the Harris County jail. Their work with our clients assure when they leave our custody they have exit plans, recovery plans, and their life plans are mapped out for them.

Another component of the program is providing services to those victims who have been caught up in criminal activity by following them to State jail where I continue to work with them there and offer continued support even after they have been released.

Not all who have begun the process are willing to go into in-patient facilities. Some wish to remain employed and support their children or family while still attending out-patient treatment options. Based upon my experience I have found that treatment is providing a success rate of up to 85 percent.

It needs to be noted that some of this population will experience a few bumps in their road to success, we also must understand that is to be expected. It is absolutely essential that we fund beds for those who have been identified as victims of international or domestic human trafficking. This group is far too familiar with conning, manipulation, lying, stealing, and cheating. My experience has shown that the majority of them express sincere guilt about crimes they were forced to commit and want to stop this endless loop but don't know how.

Hurt people hurt other people. What does human trafficking look like? Not all of these victims have criminal histories. They come from every race, gender, age, and ethnicity imaginable. The fact is, the face of international and domestic human trafficking has multiple faces, and unfortunately, we are introduced to many different faces on a daily basis. Many victims do not even realize they have been victims of human trafficking. Allow me to reiterate; hurt people, hurt other people.

Thirty-day substance abuse treatment programs are simply not long enough to address the social, physical, psychological, and developmental traumas that torment this population. It takes a lot more than just giving them C.A.R.E. packages of clothing and food. Their need for deprogramming, treatment, and assistance is not obligatory, it is mandatory if they are to survive.

Our goal is to stop victims of human trafficking from recidivating back into the criminal justice system and to put them back in the population as productive members with the same unalienable rights those of us who have not victimized too often take for granted.

I am committed for the rest of my life to stay on this battlefield, educating, rehabilitating, and teaching the world to appreciate this population while helping as many as I can escape the bondage of human trafficking for the freedom to live free.

I am begging all of you to open up your hearts and minds and to help us fight this great fight, help us to save prisoners in this silent war. People should not be for sale.

I am available to speak with anyone who would be interested in first-hand information involving this epidemic. Thank you for your time and I look forward to speaking with all of you on this issue.

God bless you and may God bless the United States of America.

[Applause.]

Chairman MCCAUL. Well, God bless you too. God bless you.

Ms. GRIFFIN-TOWNSEND. Thank you.

Chairman MCCAUL. Thank you for the courage to come forward, both you and Ms. Briggs and the victims—the courage to come forward to tell these stories that are so powerful.

Ms. GRIFFIN-TOWNSEND. Chairman, can I give this to you all?

Chairman MCCAUL. Yes.

Ms. JACKSON LEE. For the record?

Chairman MCCAUL. For the record.

Ms. GRIFFIN-TOWNSEND. This was me as a victim. This is me as a victor.

[Applause.]

Chairman MCCAUL. So without objection, this will be entered into the record with unanimous consent.

[The information follows:]

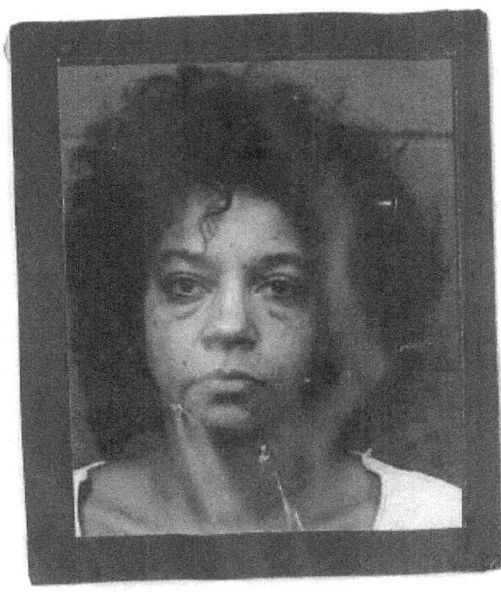

Chairman MCCAUL. Thank you for that and that will be in the Congressional record.

Ms. GRIFFIN-TOWNSEND. Oh, my God.

[Laughter.]

Chairman MCCAUL. So be careful what you ask for.

[Laughter.]

Ms. GRIFFIN-TOWNSEND. Bruised but not broken. Okay.

Chairman MCCAUL. You know, when I was deputy attorney general for criminal justice, I started the Internet Crimes Against Children Task Force. That is when I first started to get exposed to this, to see these horrific exploitations, child pornography. I think we have done some great work since then. But this issue really goes way beyond that. It is a powerful, powerful, destructive issue.

I want to again thank you for coming forward.

I have five kids, four daughters, teenage daughters, not always easy at times. I have two 12-year-old identical twin girls. When I hear the stories, when you look at the average age, and I look at these stats, and the average age of these children is 12, 13, 14 years old. The idea that they are being run through these houses and sex exploitation is I think—and I know everybody on this panel agrees—one of the most, I think, destructive, horrific acts known to mankind. We want to do everything we can in the Congress in a completely bipartisan way to stop it.

Ms. Briggs, you made an interesting comment. Children do not run to; they run from. I wanted to first ask both of you, but first Ms. Griffin-Townsend. You know, part of the problem is bringing them out of the shadows, out of the darkness and into the light, into a protected environment where they can go to law enforcement so that as my good friend, Judge Poe, states, we can put them behind bars, the people that perpetrate these horrific crimes.

How can we do a better job of getting them out of the shadows?

Ms. GRIFFIN-TOWNSEND. Mr. Chairman, the sad part about the children that end up falling prey to this population—a lot of them think that these are their boyfriends and they have been convinced and brainwashed and coerced to believing that these men and women love them. I am finding that children, when sexually molested, are—it is all molestation because they are kids and these are adults that are doing it—they think that that makes them adult. It is very hard. I have worked with so many kids because they do not want to give up the pimp boyfriend—a lot of them—because, see, there are so many hidden handcuffs and chains. A lot of them do not have the physical chains. They are invisible. This is the population that I come across all the time. Everybody is not kept in a basement. Everybody is not fed crumbs of bread and walked around on dog leashes like some of the people that I have had to work with to rehabilitate.

When you said you had twin daughters, I cringed because the thought and the fact of two 12-year-old twins—that is double the money. There is a big market for your babies. The cold part of it is they could get to your babies because of your position and try to extort you just to get them back and then they will feel, well, he is a politician, so he is not going to want anything to be exposed. Oh, my God. Believe it or not. Everybody sitting up there on that panel that has children are at greater risk because they feel they can get more money for your babies.

Then a lot of people have thought for a long time is just the throwaways, like the doctor was saying. It is anybody, and little boys bring more money than little girls.

Then we think about it. Why does it happen? If stuff is happening in the home—and when I say hurt people hurt other people, a lot of the parents were broken, and there are just generational curses that have been passed on and these secrets, and children run away from that. Then they meet somebody and they will tell them I love you, I am going to suit you up and boot you up, and you are going to have this, and you are going to have that. I promise to put you in a video, the internet, and these selfie pictures and Face Time, Instagram. Oh, my God. We are battling a lot of stuff.

Then you get addicted just as bad to the games. They will sit them down and give them PlayStations, which will traumatize them, paralyze them, and hypnotize them to tell them I am going to buy you this game and they sit there for hours. Well, that is what a lot of them were used to because parents are letting these technology games raise the children. Oh, my God. I could go on and on, Chairman.

I just wanted to come home and let you know this is happening next door, in your house, around the corner. It is everywhere.

Chairman MCCAUL. Thank you.

Ms. Briggs, I want to give you the opportunity to say something.

Ms. BRIGGS. I think that education, not necessarily of the children, but the children's parents is absolutely vital and critical. I do not think we have to reinvent the wheel. We have the DARE program in our schools already, and we need to add an element of human trafficking education from kindergarten through 12th grade. This has to be a topic that we are willing to talk about.

When I was a child, my mother was a domestic violence victim. There were no shelters to help her. So when she left, she had $13, and she left to try to find a safe place to go so that at some point she could get us kids because she had no support. So now everybody talks about domestic violence. We are talking about child abuse. We are talking about incest, and all that stuff is no longer a family issue. This has to go right up there through that process.

I think the other thing is that when did it become okay to have throwaway children. I mean, that whole term just kind of like makes my stomach sick because what does that indicate, and we continue to identify them as throwaway children. There are no throwaway people. Not in America there is not supposed to be.

You know, we need emergency shelters for these runaways where they can not get necessarily put in the juvenile justice system or CPS. Maybe we need some emergency protected safe houses for these kids at least to be able to have an opportunity to make contact with someone who might help identify the problem they were having at home before they left.

Now, the other thing that I think is very crucial for us to know is that I was on the internet and I was watching a little video. An FBI agent. There was a guy. He just got sentenced I think to two Federal life sentences for human trafficking in Federal court. So we know no parole, no good time, no nothing. So he was going to be in prison for the rest of his life. When he got done and he was coming out of the courtroom, there was an FBI agent and he had a camera set up, and he said, hey, you mind? Will you talk to me? The guy said, sure. What are you going to do? Give me life? So she said, you know, I got a question. She said, where do you get your girls? He goes, I go to the mall. He said I walked up to a little girl and I said, baby, you have beautiful eyes. If she says thank you, I just keep walking. I walk up to the next little girl and I go, baby, your hair is amazing. If she looks down and looks up and says, you really think so, he said I will leave the mall with that child willingly.

So this is not even about stranger danger. I can sit in The Woodlands where I live at the mall on any Sunday around 11:30 and watch car after car after car after car drop off their children to a safe mall in a safe neighborhood. But the more sophisticated that this crime becomes, the more education they get on what children need at specific ages. What are the struggles of development they are going through? Identity crisis. They reject everything their family is. They want to figure out who they are and they know how to work that.

So as parents, we think, okay, well, my daughter is in the bedroom. She is safe. She is in my house. But guess what? She is on the internet unsupervised where there are 50,000 predators looking for her in any day. They look for that little girl who is having a hard time or that little boy.

Thank you for mentioning little boys because in the United States we have less than 20 beds for minor boys, and minor boys are trafficked for sex between 9 and 11. The only place that they really have to go as they begin to grow up into teens is the LGBT community. I thank God that they are there. But these children need to be in a place that is not pushing them or influencing them in any direction. They are children. They do not have to make that decision today. They are carrying shame from the rapes and the homosexual rapes and acts that happened upon them that they were told that they deserved, that they were made for, that they were good at. So, No. 1, even though we always talk about girls and women, we need to never forget these are boys as well. These are men as well.

The average lifespan of a child prostitute is 7 years. When they make it to 18, it is a miracle.

The other thing is—one more thing is that what I have encountered over and over again working with the adult population is that I have had a lot of women in different places that I go and do awareness presentations. The main thing they say to me is, you know, Cheryl, she is 18 and she is standing on the corner. Ain't nobody holding a gun to her head. Now, if that was me and I was being trafficked, I would just start running and go get some help. I just say, yeah, where would you go?

Well, guess what? There are things called psychological guns. If your life is about pain and rape and beatings and exploitation, but the only good thing that you can do to continue to do that is save your little sister from being taken, that is honor. If the only thing that that victim can do is keep her family safe, she will endure it. That is honor. That is the only honor she has in her life. But she sacrifices. In many situations, they sacrifice for somebody else. Now, that does not mean they are compliant.

I remember the moment when I had the realization—and I may cry when I say this. When I was 13½ and I was where I was at and I remember thinking nobody is coming for me. Nobody knows where to look. Nobody is coming. What I want to say to you is when we have worked with rescued victims, the first thing I want them to hear is we did not forget about you. We are here. We came.

So it is not stranger danger. It is your children in the mall half-dressed, and a guy wants something. He goes, hey, I was at that concert. Where were you sitting? Did you not like the laser light show? It is all about non-threatening behavior. They are trained in how to manipulate our children and they exploit them.

So we have to start this education at K–12, and we have to have the parents involved. We got to quit thinking that it is the underprivileged minority children that it is happening to. It is everybody.

[Applause.]

Chairman MCCAUL. Well, my time has expired. But thank you so much for coming forward with that story.

I just want to end with Dr. Isaac. My time has expired, but I would like to follow up with you in terms of—perhaps later. You are kind of on the front lines with these kids coming through the hospitals, how to properly identify them and help them get out of this cycle that Ms. Briggs talks about where they can get out of that cycle and go to law enforcement.

So anyway, with that, the Chairman now recognizes the Ranking Member, Ms. Jackson Lee.

Ms. JACKSON LEE. Mr. Chairman, I think this has been one of the most powerful hearings that any of us as Members of Congress have had the privilege in serving the people of the United States of America to be a part of. We do a lot of work in Washington, DC, and sometimes the images are not of collaboration. I hope this story right here in Houston, Texas that travels all the way to the United States Congress highlights the Members and the collaborative voice of outrage, of tears. Although, Ms. Briggs, you may not hear it in our voice, see it, but it is a painful experience, but it is an important experience through you and through the other witnesses to learn the truth and then be able to act vigorously without ceasing to find answers.

Again, Mr. Chairman, I would like to offer up and mention Jacqueline Simosky.

But I would like to ask unanimous consent to put the "Slavery Today Journal", a multidisciplinary journal of human trafficking in the record. I ask unanimous consent to put this document.

Chairman MCCAUL. Without objection, so ordered.*

Ms. JACKSON LEE. I hold this up because our initial panel with excellent law enforcement—I think when we concluded, they felt no shame to be able to intermingle, Dr. Sanborn, the idea of human trafficking and slavery, modern-day slavery.

Mr. Chairman, a few years ago, I sat on the ground at the border of Bangladesh with girls who had been sold by their parents because of their devastating poverty into human trafficking and slavery. I sat on the ground. These girls were numb. They were young. I thought I am going to work to stop this in Bangladesh. Now, this was many years ago.

Here we have come thousands of miles, and I think what this panel is saying is wake up, America. Clarion call. Whether it is domestic or international—and I do not think we should distinguish except Homeland Security has this rightful position in dealing with international border security issues or issues of our border. We should not separate it. We have a global but we have a domestic—but as someone said in the earlier panel, they can be exported out and in, imported in, exported out.

Dr. Sanborn, a striking statement or report that your Children at Risk organization—and thank you for your service, and thank you for working with me for a house for the ages of 18 to 21. In that instance, it was foster care. Now I am going to embrace this larger issue because the fact is we do not have anything here in Houston to speak of, but I think it is an example of the United States.

You said every three runaways in Texas is lured into sex trafficking in 48 hours. Expand on that, and where do they go?

Mr. SANBORN. Well, across the United States, about a million children run away from home, and we know that between 150,000 and 300,000 of those young girls—probably about the fourth time that they run away, they are lured into trafficking. When you run away from home the third or fourth time, you are going to go somewhere a little bit farther away. So maybe you take the bus to the nearest big city, the nearest big, warm climate city. That might be Dallas, Atlanta, San Diego, and many places in Houston, especially for girls from the middle of the country, Louisiana, Mississippi. Houston is a big destination. They arrive at the bus station, and

---

*Slavery Today Journal, Vol. 1, Issue 1, February 2014. The information has been retained in committee files and is available at http://www.slaverytodayjournal.org/downloads/february-full-issue-2014/.

85

the bus station is a place where a lot of these traffickers will look
for these girls. A cute little 12-year-old coming off the bus—they
are very approachable for a free meal at McDonald's and expansion
beyond that. Sometimes these girls very quickly, as Kathy and
Cheryl will tell you, within a number of days, they are selling
themselves because they have fallen in love, quote/unquote, with
this trafficker.

Ms. JACKSON LEE. Would you say that every day a child is getting off a bus somewhere or hitchhiking? I do not know how popular that is. So as we sit here today, could there be someone getting off a bus and being enticed in the wrong direction?

Mr. SANBORN. I would say every day there are many girls that
get off buses in many places that are lured into trafficking. You
know, the shame of it is for many domestic victims today, Congresswoman, that if we were to go on the internet where many of
these or most of these young domestic victims are sold now, it
would be faster to get a young girl delivered to us, faster than getting a pizza delivered. It is a shame, and this is happening in
Houston a lot, and it is a shame for us. Shame on us as a city.

Ms. JACKSON LEE. My commitment to you that we may make—
this may be the epicenter of human trafficking, but it is going to
be the paradise of refuge for children. We are going to find a way
to break the barriers.

[Applause.]

Ms. JACKSON LEE. I know my colleagues—some are from Houston. The Chairman is not except for the fact that his district over-
laps.

We thank you very much. But I think we can be an example in
this city.

Dr. Isaac, I went out at night with one of our agencies that deals
with runaways. So I went out at night to find them. This is a warm
city, but I went out to find them on streets in a cold time.

You talked about health care, and obviously young women need
their own gynecological treatment or medical treatment, young
men. My question is what in Congress on the medical side could
we do?

I just noted that HHS, since 2009, has spent all of their appropriations that we have given them—obviously, too little—before the
end of the appropriations term. That means that for a period of
time in the United States, we have no impact on certain areas in
terms of helping these children. What can we do with respect to the
medical part of it?

Dr. ISAAC. The medical part of it. As I stated, I believe it is the
education of some of our health care professionals. A lot of them
may see these children, and they are very rough-and-tumbled children. Again, they are children. I have certainly seen kids who have
come through the emergency room. They certainly do not cooperate
sometimes with our exams. But I usually tell them to have them
come within 24 or 48 hours to our medical clinic that deals specifically—again, this is at the Children's Assessment Center if you are
in Harris County—to come within 24 or 48 hours to come to our
clinic. Within that time, these are children who are very pliable.
This is time that they have been away from their traffickers, that
they have had their change of mind. They are completely pliable

and cooperative with the exam and giving their historical histories of what has happened. It is very intriguing to see that a lot of these kids I will see, when I turn my back—they are actually reading books to the other little kids. So they are essentially children. So, again, it is the education of our health care professionals.

As I said also, we have a system and a project that we are working on that is directed to educating these workers to identify and interview these children.

Ms. JACKSON LEE. I understand my colleague, Mr. Poe, has to leave in just a second. So let me just quickly—these are the two witnesses that I wanted to probe. So let me just quickly ask Ms. Briggs and Ms. Griffin-Townsend, first of all, if love could pour from the table, it would be going to all of you here at this table. To those who are courageous enough to be here with the reflection of all the other sisters and brothers that may not be able to be here, we thank them for their courage and all of you.

Just very, very quickly. I am so glad that the two of you have said, "I am a prostitute, or was. How dare you denigrate me? How dare you consider me someone who is a disgrace, who is on the street, who loves sex?" Tell us what you need in order to take that to a higher level so that this prostitution issue leading into human trafficking can also be stopped immediately.

I thank the Chairman.

Ms. BRIGGS. Thank you so much, Ms. Lee.

I believe that what we really need at this point is we need funding and we need funding for emergency places for our children that have nowhere else to go where they can actually obtain resources and not be charged as a criminal or be put in a foster home that maybe not be the best situation for them.

I think the second thing that we need is we need to have required—we need to develop required minimum standards of care. In every other industry, they have them. Every other industry has a watchdog organization like JCAHO for the hospital systems and whatever it is for the forensic crime labs. In order to get funding from the State or Federal Government, they should have to pass an audit that says, hey, we have adequate services, because guess what? A warm bed and a meal ain't enough. They got to have trauma therapy. They have to have trauma-informed care. They have to have drug counseling. They got to have rehabilitation in that area. They have got to learn about—they are never going to play with Barbies again. Okay, we can forget that. But what we cannot take away from them is the adult responsibilities to figure out how they are going to care and pay for themselves. But we have to empower them.

Ms. JACKSON LEE. Thank you.

Ms. GRIFFIN-TOWNSEND. Also, Congresswoman Lee, each one of these individuals—I mean, I want to stress this. It is devastating for a child to be caught up. But the children, let me say, that are here in Houston, Texas—a lot of them do not feel that they are a victim and do not want to be rescued. I know me, you, and all of these young survivors over here—you could not tell us anything. We thought we were grown. I mean, really, we had been brainwashed or whatever. Then after you get 19 years old now, you have aged out. You are no good anymore. At 19 you are a has-been. So now the only thing you know—you are psychologically damaged. You do not know anything else but to jump in and out of cars or sell yourself on Craigslist. You know, you run into Walgreen's and steal some makeup. Then you get beat up. If you are in the strip club, if you do not give the pimp or the DJ or the manager the money, fake ID's—it is horrible. For too long people have over-looked us.

I am not proud to say that I was a drug addict and a prostitute, but I am grateful that I was able to make the decision to survive and turn that mess into this message.

Grants and all of that—you know, they have these strict qualifications. You have got to have this degree and that degree. Peer to peer. When I say you got to gain the trust at the beginning when you first get somebody—the reason why I have been able to break through the barriers is because I can show them mug shots. I can show them this broke arm and where this ear has been cut off and my face has been rebuilt. I have been dragged and I am fixing to get me a hip replacement when I get time after trying to help all these folks. I need it. I am just saying they know I have been there and I have done that. Some of these people that were in the life with me I have been able to go back and pull out. It is a domino effect. They are going to be able to go back and pull out because people need to know you know what you are talking about. I can identify with you.

So that is why I say we are basically on the front end as the colonics. We have to get them, get their trust, clean them up, and then, yes, the professionals have to be there, but do not discredit us because we are going to get their trust and get you ready to go on to those professionals and get you some real help and rehabilitation.

[Applause.]

Ms. JACKSON LEE. Thank you for letting me know all of them.

Chairman MCCAUL. The Chairman now recognizes Mr. Poe.

Mr. POE. I thank the Chairman.

There are three statements that I want to go over that you all made.

Dr. Sanborn, you said there were 20 beds in all of the United States of America for boys that are trafficked at 9 to 11. Is that what you said?

Mr. SANBORN. I think it was one of the——

Mr. POE. One of you all said that. That is a true statement. You just did not say it.

Mr. SANBORN. Yes.

Mr. POE. Who said that? Ms. Briggs? There are 20 beds.

Ms. GRIFFIN-TOWNSEND. Less than 20.

Mr. POE. Twenty beds for boys that are 9 to 11 that are trafficked in the United States.

Ms. BRIGGS. There are less than 20 beds for boys 9 to 17.

Mr. POE. Nine to 17.

Ms. BRIGGS. Yes. Out in LA, there is Children of the Night. I do believe they have 15 boys and girls spots. Then you have Isaiah's House in Montana which has 8 boys and 8 girls spots. That is all that is designated for male children victims.

Mr. POE. Do you think that is a tragedy?

88

Ms. BRIGGS. I absolutely do.

Mr. POE. In a country like this, we can only provide 30 beds for trafficked boys that are domestic trafficked boys?

Ms. BRIGGS. I really do believe that boys may carry a greater depth of shame because of the type of rape that is forced upon them. I do believe that.

It is kind of like having a guy who is a domestic violence victim. I worked at the shelter for 5 years, and very few times—I had a guy tell me when we put him and his kids up in a hotel that the police officer laughed at him and said, what do you mean your wife is beating you up? You know, you are twice as big as she is. He just did not believe in violence.

So I think it is the same thing. Boys have a hard problem self-identifying even more than any other population, and I think we need to work closely with like the Polaris Project and local hotlines and local organizations so that we can then begin to identify these boys because I promise you they are there in pretty much the same numbers as girls.

Mr. POE. Let me ask the question, Ms. Griffin-Townsend. Then you can give the answers.

You said that people should not be for sale. Do you not think that is exactly what—we need to solve that problem, that overall problem. I mean, that is the big picture. That is the humanity and what we are trying to do is making sure that people are not for sale. Those days should have ended a long time ago.

Ms. GRIFFIN-TOWNSEND. Absolutely.

Mr. POE. I know you want to say something, but I am talking right now. You are dying to say something.

I want to thank you and Ms. Briggs especially for your courage. You got a lot of wisdom that you are sharing with us. Ms. Griffin-Townsend, I want to thank you for bringing your amen corner out here today as well.

[Laughter.]

Mr. POE. The only other thing—Ms. Briggs, you do not need to comment unless you want to. You said it felt like, as a victim, nobody is coming for me. We want to change that dynamic as well. All of us working together. Children should never be in a position in life where they feel like nobody is going to look for them. Nobody is coming for them.

So I want to thank all of you for your wisdom and our experts on this end of the table. We got experts everywhere. Dr. Sanborn and Dr. Isaac, especially with Children's Assessment Center, thank you.

I yield back, Mr. Chairman.

Chairman MCCAUL. The Chair now recognizes Mr. Al Green.

Mr. AL GREEN of Texas. Thank you, Mr. Chairman.

I would like to extend my thanks to the people who testified and the people who stood by them, stood with them, helped them to get to this point. Kathy—and that is how I know you affectionately— you just celebrated a birthday.

Ms. BRIGGS. Yes, I did.

Mr. AL GREEN of Texas. You just celebrated a birthday.

Ms. BRIGGS. Thank you.

Mr. AL GREEN of Texas. But for intervention and somebody understanding that you were somebody, that you were a child of the same God that created the rich man, the same God that created the Wall Street millionaire, you are a child of that same God. But for that, you may not have celebrated that last birthday. So I am grateful that you have given your testimony, all of you.

Someone testified earlier that—they did not use this term, but I am going to use it—"the master" because there is a master-servant relationship here, master-slave relationship. Someone testified that the master makes $31,000 a week. That is what I heard. I wrote it down. Thirty-one thousand dollars a week in a small market—in a small market. Houston is not a small market. What are some of these masters making in Houston, Texas? Kathy, can you give us some insight please?

Ms. GRIFFIN-TOWNSEND. Yes, sir. By Houston being so spread out, we do not have zoning. Let me tell you. An abandoned house with no windows, weeds growing up, milk crates on the inside of the house, an old, dirty mattress on the floor can bring in as much as $35,000 to $50,000 a week.

Mr. AL GREEN of Texas. My God.

Ms. GRIFFIN-TOWNSEND. We just pass by and think them just homeless people.

You see, the corner drug dealer, the little small-time dope dealer, is just a pawn. They use him because he knows now especially all of our adult children who were just prostitutes that have aged out of all of that juvenile human trafficking and domestic and incest and molestation. They are looking at them as damaged goods. Those are the ones now that are so addicted and will do anything and anybody that will bring me a hit of any kind of dope is my savior now. So I am going to do whatever you ask me to do. Just give me some dope.

Mr. AL GREEN of Texas. That is a good segue into the second part of my question. If the master makes $30,000 to $50,000 a week, what does a servant make? What does a servant get?

Ms. GRIFFIN-TOWNSEND. Most of the little nickel-and-dime drug dealers—they are addicted to another drug. So they end up not making anything. They are doing that to get their dope. The only somebody that is winning is the master, and then the middleman gets maybe 2 grand. They are getting all of that. Or they give them a car, you know, what I am talking about, them bouncing or something like that.

VOICES. Swingers.

Ms. GRIFFIN-TOWNSEND. What did you call them?

VOICES. Swingers.

Ms. GRIFFIN-TOWNSEND. Swingers. You got a whole choir over there that can tell you exactly how it is done.

They do not even know that they are being used as slaves themselves. They do not even know it. They think that if they got $200 in their pocket, they are balling. It is so sad.

Congressman, like I say, I got to take you to the streets for real.

Mr. AL GREEN of Texas. Well, you and I have agreed that we will go to the facility that made the news yesterday and we will go to other places after that.

But I want to thank you again, Mr. Chairman. I thank all of the witnesses for appearing and just simply let you know that there are no throwaways in the America that I love.

[Applause.]

Mr. AL GREEN of Texas. Thank you and God bless you.

Chairman MCCAUL. Thank you, Al.

The Chairman now recognizes Mr. Farenthold.

Mr. FARENTHOLD. Thank you, Mr. Chairman.

Dr. Sanborn, I will start with you since we talked a little bit about the internet in the last round of questionings, and you brought up a website that advertises some of these services. Would shutting down those sites make a difference, or would they just pop back up internationally where we could not get to them? How do we do it without casting an over-broad net that would violate the First Amendment?

Mr. SANBORN. I think that is a great question.

Please do not ever put me on a panel with Cheryl and Kathy again.

[Laughter.]

Mr. SANBORN. I am not used to being a sidekick.

You know, it is a very tricky question, is it not, because most of the business has moved to the internet, but there are a lot of people that are hiding behind the First Amendment. I am a big believer in the First Amendment and we have lots of lawyers on our staff that would say we are all behind the First Amendment. You are right. If we decided today to shut down backpage.com, there would be others that people would move to. But the fact of the matter is we need to just keep shutting them down.

When Craigslist was pressured into being shut down, what we found is that some of these purchasers were lost for a little while until they found backpage.com. There is no way that backpage.com is going to do the same thing that Craigslist did, which is to shut down on its own, because it is making way too much money. It is owned by the *Village Voice* and it is making a lot of money. They recently separated from the *Village Voice,* but they were making a lot of money.

Mr. AL GREEN of Texas. So let me go on and talk a little bit. You know, I asked our law enforcement folks on the last panel, why do you not just go on this website and go into each and every one of those organizations and rescue the victims? He said, well, it was a matter of setting priorities. I fell into that trap with him. I said, yes, well, I guess, you know going after murderers is a priority. Then I got to think beyond murder or plotting terrorism, holding young children in basic slavery—I cannot think of a higher priority.

[Applause.]

Mr. FARENTHOLD. But I fell into that trap.

I heard for years from folks, you know, prostitution is a victimless crime. Ms. Briggs, how many are there because they want to be there? Are there any?

Ms. BRIGGS. I have never in my life met one woman who, if you offered her—or child, if you offered them a viable second option, who would continue to do what they are having to do for survival.

Mr. FARENTHOLD. We talked a little bit about the customers here and what we could do about the customers. Let me ask you: Do the customers even know that the person that they are hiring may be—I am using air quotes for "hiring"—is there involuntarily? Do they know whether or not they are a 14-year-old?

Ms. GRIFFIN-TOWNSEND. Yes and they do not care.

Mr. FARENTHOLD. So you think going after the demand, as Judge Poe said, would make a huge, huge difference.

Ms. BRIGGS. Right, because if you cut down the amount of people out there buying sex, then a pimp that has seven girls—if he can only sell five of those on a daily basis, he is going to let two go. So that is the deal: Supply and demand, supply and demand. It is international.

Mr. FARENTHOLD. So how do we convince the law enforcement community that this needs to be a higher priority? I mean, there are things we can do in Congress. We can rewrite the laws to broaden some of the definitions that we have talked about. We can change some of the language with visas that we have talked about. But when it comes down to it, it is up to the law enforcement folks on the street to make that a priority.

What do we do besides have hearings like this, talk to the television cameras? Are we doing everything we can do? I am going to let Ms. Griffin-Townsend answer that.

Ms. GRIFFIN-TOWNSEND. The first piece is to get a room full of survivors—there are many—and put us all in front of law enforcement and look at what the real faces of this travesty actually look like.

[Applause.]

Ms. GRIFFIN-TOWNSEND. Stop being ashamed. Stop being embarrassed because, you know, how many get to live two lifetimes in one lifetime? All of us have and we can pass that on and let them know that. Then everybody has got something that they want to keep secret that they do not want God to know, but he already knows. You can keep yours held, but we need to bring it out and show them the different real basis of it so they will know what to go after because everybody is keeping it in a little box. This thing is bigger than a box. There is no such thing as a box when it comes to this sexual slavery.

Mr. FARENTHOLD. Well, hopefully, this hearing will take a step towards that. There were a lot of cameras here earlier. Hopefully, the coverage that we get tonight from this will be one step in making a difference in people's lives.

I applaud what you are doing, helping folks one person at a time. Again, I applaud you, and God bless you.

[Applause.]

Chairman MCCAUL. Thanks.

Let me just close by saying I have chaired a lot of hearings. This has been the most powerful. We deal with a lot of threats. We deal with al-Qaeda, terrorist threats, but this is the biggest threat to our children right here in the United States. We have an obligation to do something about that.

As Sheila talked about earlier, we do a lot of stuff up there that does not amount to anything, but this is an area where we can really, truly make a difference in the lives of others and our most vulnerable in our society. We want to change lives from this to this side and that is our goal.

[Applause.]

Chairman MCCAUL. As you said—and I will not filibuster here, but you said we want to turn that mess into a message. Wow. That is a powerful message and it is a powerful message that we need to send back to Washington and work this thing out on both sides of the aisle, which is not happening enough today in Washington, make this thing work not for us but for these children that are being exploited and for you, the victims. We owe this to you.

I just want to really thank all the panelists but particularly the victims for the courage to come out in the open, come out of the shadows and say, you know what? I am somebody and I deserve to be heard. We want you all to do something to stop this from happening again. So all I can say is thank you.

I want to give you credit also for working with me to do this field hearing right here in your district and want to give you the opportunity to give the final word.

Ms. JACKSON LEE. Mr. Chairman, the hearts of Members were exposed today, and what you heard was not a Chairman of a distinguished background, a law enforcement background, but you heard a father. You heard a man with a heart. You saw the best of what Congress is and can be. We are all on one page. We all have cracking voices, watery eyes. I think that we have now opened with a flashlight and we are looking for sunlight to be able to shine on victims that are human beings to be loved.

I love what all my Members have said and your testimony. Can you believe this has been happening to children? It is not because of our benign neglect. It is because of what is your priority, what are you thinking of. So today, in an official Congressional hearing, the first hearing in Houston on human trafficking brought people together that I think will be the light of America and the light of the world. Let us touch somebody and say that you are valuable and I will not view you in any other way than the valuable person that you are. This human trafficking hearing has exposed slavery and human trafficking and smuggling, and we have said one thing. You are all the same and we are going to get you. I am grateful that we are going to do it in a bipartisan manner based on heart and love and the values of this great Nation.

Mr. Chairman, thank you so much for your courtesy.

Chairman MCCAUL. We thank you.

[Applause.]

Chairman MCCAUL. Let me just say this hearing is adjourned, but our mission has just begun.

[Whereupon, at 1:04 p.m., the committee was adjourned.]

○

www.ingramcontent.com/pod-product-compliance
Lightning Source LLC
Chambersburg PA
CBHW081840280526
45789CB00007B/2519